Fintech is the Future

The Perfect Business for Anyone to Build Wealth and Bless People At the Same Time!

Reco M. McCambry, MBA

All rights reserved. No part of this book may be used, reproduced, or transmitted in any manner whatsoever including electronic, mechanical, photocopying, recording, or any information storage and retrieval system without written permission of the publisher or author.

Contact the author or publisher if you would like information about how to access any and all programs or other materials associated with this book and its contents.

This book may be purchased for educational, business, sales, or promotional use. For information or to order, please contact:

Email: info@FintechIsTheFuture.com
Website: www.FintechIsTheFuture.com
Office: (678) 379-7211
Fax: (678) 528-9513

1506 Klondike Rd SW
Ste 403
Conyers, GA 30094

Copyright © 2025 by Reco M. McCambry, MBA

Table of Contents

Other Books by Reco M. McCambry	IV
Disclaimer	V
Introduction	VI
1. The Top 5 Causes of Poverty & Economic Inequality	1
2. The Rise of Fintech	22
3. How Fintech Equalizes Access to Capital	40
4. How Fintech Can Improve Financial Education	58
5. How Fintech Can Help You Build Credit	74
6. How Fintech Gives You Access to Opportunity	108
7. How Fintech Can Help Solve The Debt Crisis	128
8. How Can You Profit from Fintech While Blessing Others?	140
9. How Can Fintech Reshape the Future?	164
10. About the Author	168

Other Books by Reco M. McCambry

The Fatherless Father

The Plan After Police Reform That Will Guarantee Social Justice and Progress for the Black Community

The Plan After Police Reform That Will Guarantee Social Justice and Progress for the Black Community: Participatory Workbook

Disclaimer

The information provided in this book is for informational purposes only and is not intended to be a source of advice or credit analysis with respect to the material presented. The information in this book does not constitute financial advice, as individual situations vary, and the financial landscape can change rapidly.

The publisher and the author do not make any guarantee or other promise as to any results that may be obtained from using the content of this book. You should never make any investment decision without first conducting your own research and due diligence. The author and publisher accept no responsibility for the actions of readers, as we cannot control these actions.

The information contained in this book is complete and accurate to the best of the author and publisher's knowledge as of this writing in December of 2024. However, because global financial markets and finance laws can change rapidly, it is highly recommended that the reader conduct their own due diligence research at the time of reading before making major decisions.

Introduction

We live in uncertain times. That has always been true, but it is *especially* true in the 21st century, when our powerful technology has the potential to transform the world, for better or worse, and we can feel powerless to influence how technology is used by corporations. At this moment, we are staring down the barrel of mass job loss due to automation, combined with a trend of increasing wealth inequality that has been accelerating for nearly 50 years.

This book is a message of hope. In it, we will show how you can use cutting-edge financial technology in a rapidly growing industry to create financial security for your family, and how you can do it while making the world a better, more egalitarian place.

Who am I to be telling you such things? I'm Reco McCambry, founder, President and CEO of Novae. Our business model is simply this: we profit by providing financial education and fintech solutions to consumers and small business owners in traditionally underserved communities nationwide.

Are you surprised that there's money in this? Don't be. Since time immemorial, it's been the people of the working classes who work the hardest. Much of wealth and income inequality has come from the ability of those who are already powerful to exploit that labor and keep its profits for themselves.

The rich don't actually *make* the most money, and they never have. Wealth is created by labor which creates value, whether it is the labor of farmers, miners, factory or warehouse workers, retail workers, artisans, inventors, or scientists. Power structures have depended simply on those who already have money being able to take credit for the labor of the workers they control.

And financial technology, also known as fintech, has the potential to disrupt all of that.

I grew up in a city called McDonough, Georgia, and lived in a couple of housing projects early in life. No one in my family had ever been educated about business or finance, and I believe that was intentional. There's a reason why public schools never taught students about business, investing, or other vehicles for making and growing wealth rapidly until quite recently (I'm told a few schools do teach these subjects now).

The knowledge about how to access financing, turn financing into profit, and invest those profits so that your wealth grows along with the world market has historically been restricted to rich families. Just as Robert Kiyosaki explains in his ultra-bestselling book, *Rich Dad, Poor Dad*, much of the difference between wealth and poverty comes down to financial education.

That was something I sure didn't grow up with. But I was fortunate enough to have two chance encounters that changed my life.

One was my introduction to the direct selling industry. One of the best-kept secrets of our economy is that sales is probably the world's most lucrative profession. We don't see sales professionals as being on par with C-suite executives, and sometimes they're not; but sometimes they are.

Selling is, after all, the single most valuable service an employee can offer a company. Making sales is the basis of all business. For that reason, companies often reward sales professionals in direct proportion to how good they are at selling. Sales professionals are often paid on commission, which means that those who sell high-ticket products and get very good at it can earn hundreds of thousands of dollars per year in sales commissions, and sometimes even millions!

To be honest, I think most people don't take an interest in the sales profession because it sounds too good to be true. It's hard for many people who were raised to expect a five-figure salary at best to believe that they could really sell millions of dollars of products or a multimillion dollar property and receive a ten percent commission on it *regularly*. For people accustomed to being paid a salary worth a small fraction of the real value of their labor, it feels like cheating or unrealistic.

But it is sustainable. After I began selling as an independent direct sales professional as a side hustle during college, I quickly realized this could become a career much more lucrative than any college degree would give me.

Direct sales is the art and business of connecting products with customers who want and need them, by being an intermediary between the product and the customer, without owning the product. It is the essential piece that happens between the design of a product and its enjoyment by a consumer. The digital era is especially fertile with direct sales opportunities, due to the many opportunities to use digital technology to connect people to existing resources.

Here are some examples of well-known businesses that specialize in this practice of connecting products to their customers, without the immense expense of having to own or create the products themselves:

- Uber made $37 billion in 2023 by offering driving services to customers—without owning any cars.

- Visa made $32 billion in 2023 by connecting people with loans and credit lines—without owning a traditional bank.

- Spotify made $14 billion in 2023 by connecting listeners with music—without owning a recording studio.

- Expedia made $12 billion in 2023 by connecting travelers to travel deals—without owning a single hotel or airplane.

The second discovery I was blessed to realize was during my journey to get my MBA in my 30s. I did a case study about the emergence of new opportunities in the fintech industry, and this led to a lifelong research path.

I'd grown up in a desperately underbanked area: that's a term for neighborhoods where banks frankly don't bother to set up bank branches because they don't think there's enough money to be made. As a result, many people in my town grew up knowing little about what banks could offer them. For those of us who did learn what we were missing out on, it was depressing and infuriating to be overlooked and denied those opportunities.

Underbanking is a huge cause of inequality, since people without access to banks can't get good loans, grants, mortgages, or invest in the stock market. Underbanking, therefore, is a huge reason why the poor stay poor while the rich get richer. I wanted to know what the advancing technology of software and the Internet could do to make banking and financing more accessible to people like me, who grew up in towns with almost no bank branches or access to financial services that were essential to building a solid financial future.

What I found shocked me. Financial technology, even a decade ago in the late 2010s, had the power to almost completely remove many barriers to financial services and financial education. There was no technical reason why anyone in America with a smartphone *couldn't* learn how to build credit history and then actually do it, concluding the process by obtaining a low-interest business loan or qualifying for a home loan, helping them get on track to realize their dreams.

There was no reason at all why that couldn't happen every day. Except that no one had developed the business model for it yet. So

I did.

When creating Novae, I combined the direct sales business model that had worked so well for me and my wife Shaneé with the astounding potential of financial technology to serve underserved communities. We started out with a simple proposition: our direct sales force would sell financial education and credit-building products to people across the country, with a special interest in underserved communities. The people we served would have much greater access to financial services. They would know how to qualify for the financial products that every American family needs the most.

We built up our customer base in more ways than one. Our customers would become financially smarter as a result of working with us. That made the product easier to sell, and created interest in what else we could do to keep making our customers advancing financially. That led to the Novae of today, which has now been on the Inc 5000 list of fastest-growing businesses in America for four years running. And the business didn't exist before 2014.

Iam not telling you all this to sell you Novae; I am telling you this to sell you on your own power. By understanding fintech and seeing how it could serve the underserved, allowing the hardest-working people in our society to keep the profits of their own labor, I was able to build a multi-million dollar and an Inc 5000 company within six years of starting.

Fintech is still in its relative infancy. Major financial institutions have been slow to take advantage of its opportunities, affected by the inertia of old business models and skepticism of new technologies. This is great news for me: the relative lack of competition has been a major reason why Novae has been able to grow so fast. And it means that your fintech business could grow fast, too, if you get in during this golden window of market undersaturation.

So what can you do by understanding the power of fintech?

In this book, we will explore some of the most important financial technology tools that are available to consumers and business owners today. We'll examine ways that fintech can make business owners rich and create financial relief and stability even for consumers who do not plan to start their own business. Indeed, these two populations are intimately intertwined: fintech business owners can get rich by helping consumers to get out of debt, qualify for financing to own a home or get a loan to start a business, and more.

We'll see how fintech models offering debt settlement are helping to alleviate America's debt crisis (and will probably grow rapidly over the next decade as the crisis continues), how fintech can be used to fight the failures and abuses of America's financial system, and how remote banking and financial education can allow anyone with a smartphone to start a profitable business with millionaire potential in the fintech industry.

Sound too good to be true? So did direct sales. So did the untapped potential of fintech, when I first began learning about it. If something sounds too good to be true, maybe it's because you've been conditioned to accept less. Maybe you have been conditioned to believe that good things are impossible for you.

Direct sales made my wife and I both millionaires in our 20s.

INTRODUCTION

This didn't happen because we came from privilege. As African Americans, we came from families that were enslaved only a few centuries ago. I spent part of my childhood in public housing projects; she spent part of hers in a trailer park, both of us raised by single mothers. To be honest, we were very limited in our activities and expectations growing up because our families lacked resources.

In my lifetime, God has blessed my family to experience things that generations before it would have only imagined. We were blessed to discover the direct sales business model in our early 20s and the potential of fintech to create systems that fight inequality in our late 30s.

I believe that God blesses us so that we can bless others. Novae is my best attempt to create a business and a business model that allows others to not only profit, but to learn skills that will help them to be wealthy and empowered throughout their lives. And this book is my best attempt to educate you about the power of financial education, and how the rapidly advancing field of financial technology can help you and others, both as customers and as entrepreneurs.

Fintech changes the way money moves. This has great potential for either good or evil. I am here to encourage you to fight for good in the field of fintech—and to change your own fortune for the better as you do it. This book begins to lay out what I believe is the best way to get started.

I invite you to come with me now as we discuss how financial technology can solve some of our world's biggest problems by empowering those who have historically been disempowered. Whether you are urban or rural, and regardless of what trade or profession you're skilled in, fintech can set you on the path to financial security and prosperity if used wisely.

And I will do my best to give you the knowledge that you can't afford *not* to have in this economy.

So read on, and let's change the world for the better. God knows the world needs it.

Chapter 1

The Top 5 Causes of Poverty & Economic Inequality

We live in an exciting era. Many of the historic "unavoidable" causes of poverty have been eradicated. With advancing technology, the global economy now produces more than enough to house and feed everyone well. So where does poverty come from in a world like this one?

The buzzword of this century will be "access." Enough food and other resources exist to ensure that no one has to live in poverty; but systems do not yet exist to distribute wealth and survival necessities to those who need them. This is in part due to a shortage of physical infrastructure to move physical goods, like food and housing supplies, around the world. But it's also due to economic and legal systems that were created to perpetuate inequality and ensure that most opportunities went to people who were already rich.

You've heard versions of this same old story many times in history class. It shows up in obvious places like redlining, where historically only certain types of people were allowed to buy nice houses in good neighborhoods. But you've probably heard far less about the barriers within our financial and educational systems that continue to perpetuate inequality by making it more difficult for children of poor families to access capital and financial education than children of rich families.

It's important to note that this kind of inequality is not *just* dangerous to those living in poverty. Money has a powerful effect on politics, and societies with higher levels of wealth inequality tend to have less effective democracies and more violent and bigoted political behavior.

Money in politics can also seriously affect decisions about the funding and administration of programs like public schools, healthcare, housing, childcare, higher education, and universal basic income. Politicians and campaign donors who have never been poor are likely to vote against funding public services that they see as "unnecessary" because their families were able to pay for everything for them, and against regulations that lower the costs of amenities like housing and medical care.

This means that wealth inequality can rapidly become self-reinforcing and self-perpetuating, as wealthy politicians and political donors vote to defund programs that their families don't need, but which most citizens of their societies *do* need to remain housed, educated, and in good health. Taken to an extreme, this can even cause nation collapse as most citizens no longer see a reason to support the nation or government that has not supported their basic needs.

The role of finance and wealth distribution in a society can't be underestimated. Too often, who has access to finance and wealth determines what a country's laws will be, what human rights its citizens will enjoy, how long they will live, and the quality of life they enjoy. I believe God calls us to take positive action in these realms, and this is why I have made it Novae's mission to tear down these barriers to wealth and finance inequality.

By using digital technology and financial technology strategically, we can overcome *most* barriers to finance access for people of all backgrounds. And you can too. This is an area that is rife with opportunities for entrepreneurship, and companies like mine even provide education about how you can capitalize on these opportunities to gain wealth while also helping others.

So how exactly do we do that? Throughout this chapter, I want to explain in detail the top five causes of wealth inequality in the United States today. As we discuss each cause, we will also discuss how financial technology offers a solution—and how any person who wants to change their life, and the lives of others, can make money while helping others to do the same.

#1 Barrier to Equality: *Access to Financial Education*

You don't know what you don't know. This is why education is the first hurdle to jump when you want to do literally anything. You can't do something if you don't know how; you can't even begin to put the necessary tools or strategy in place to accomplish your goal if you don't know precisely how such a goal is accomplished.

This is a major barrier that has historically kept the children of non-rich parents from becoming rich. As Robert Kiyosaki explained in his ultra-bestselling book *Rich Dad, Poor Dad*, wealthy parents teach their children *very* different things about finance than low-income parents. For that matter, public schools also generally don't touch the kind of financial education that children of wealthy families receive from their elders.

Did you know, for example, that most wealthy people *don't* use their own money to fund their businesses? Instead, they know how to obtain huge, low-interest loans and credit lines.

Imagine having tens of thousands of dollars at your fingertips to fund any business you might wish to start: that is the benefit that wealthy people who are raised with knowledge of how to build credit history, qualify for excellent loans, and then build a business that pays back their loan *and* makes them wealthy in their own right have access to.

In many cases, it is not access to a family's wealth that allows children of wealthy families to start wildly successful businesses. Having family wealth can save children of wealthy families if they make bad decisions, but more often than not, the businesses are actually started with loans or other forms of borrowed capital. It is the *knowledge* of how to qualify for and obtain those loans which allows these startup owners to be successful.

This was the earliest work Novae did. We used digital technology to teach people from across the country how to qualify for the best loans, and how to use them. Part of our success occurred because our customers themselves started to become more financially educated and successful; they had money to buy other products and services from us. In this way, we are incentivized to get excellent outcomes for our customers; the smarter and more wealthy our customers become, the more our company can grow.

Some of you might point out that there is likely some degree of discrimination involved in the decisions made by certain financial institutions. And you are right. There are some financial institutions which likely give better treatment to children of wealthy families, even if other factors such as credit history and business plans are equal.

This is another way in which fintech can actually help. When loan applications are conducted online, or even automated, human discrimination does not enter the mix. If your loan officer never sees your face, how can they discriminate on a basis of race or another matter of appearance? If your approval is conducted by an algorithm which only analyzes the credit history you have built and does not see how you are dressed or where you live, it cannot discriminate against you.

There are very real concerns that AI and remote approvals can still include elements of discrimination, but these can be controlled for. The designers of algorithms decide what variables their algorithms take into account, and we at Novae and our fintech partners, for example, are able to build ours to be completely blind to all factors other than an applicant's credit history.

We are hopeful that other institutions will follow our example as remote and automated financial decisions become more common—and as our competition sees how wildly we succeed by choosing to approve loans for people without regard for their race, class, age, or other factors which are ultimately irrelevant to their work ethic and likelihood of success in business.

By making detailed, practical financial knowledge accessible to anyone, anywhere with an Internet connection and a smartphone, and making loans and other forms of financing accessible in the same way, fintech has the potential to lower the most important barriers to wealth, including those which have been used historically to perpetuate and increase inequality.

#2 Barrier to Equality: Access to Capital

Let's take a quick moment to discuss what "capital" is. In short, capital is money—it means having access to the necessary funds to get something done. Our economic system is called "capitalism" because what happens in our society is primarily determined by who has capital and how they use it.

In theory, capitalism creates a meritocracy with high social mobility—the ability to make money and gain status through hard work, regardless of your parents' wealth or social status. This is supposed to happen because people who are skilled and hard-working earn money by providing goods and services that people want and are willing to pay for.

However, this principle doesn't work and capitalism doesn't

produce social mobility when economic inequality exists. If only the privileged class has access to capital, or if big businesses can accumulate the financial capital to put all competition out of business, then capitalism no longer produces social mobility and meritocracy.

In fact, when monopolies and education inequality interfere with competition and meritocracy, the quality and quantity of goods and services available in a society go down. This is because those who control the capital no longer have to provide as many, or as high-quality services to continue being paid if they are the only service providers available to most people, especially if they already have a comfortable amount of wealth and are not being pushed to find new ways to win over more customers.

Unfortunately, this is a state our economy has gotten to. Most industries are controlled by just a handful of huge companies, which cuts back on competition and therefore on the quality and availability of goods. Extreme inequality in access to capital and financial education means that many businesses are run by people who were born rich, and were therefore able to buy out small business owners or outcompete them.

Fintech has the potential to make real changes in this situation by equalizing access to capital. How can it do that?

We have already discussed how lack of access to financial education results in economic inequality. People who aren't taught how to build credit, how to get home and business loans and other forms of financing, how to invest money to grow their wealth passively, etc. are far more likely to remain poor and far less likely to end up running a thriving business than people who are taught to do those things by their families or expensive private schools.

But even if someone *knows* how to build credit history and apply for loans, they may still face obstacles.

Underbanking is one important obstacle. Historically, many big banks simply did not bother to have branches in low-income neighborhoods because they did not think it was worth their time to do business with low-income clients.

Underbanking has devastating effects. A recent survey showed that only about 6% of Americans did not have a bank account; 94% of Americans did. If you have a bank account, you probably have trouble imagining how someone could possibly get by without one. Having a bank account is necessary to write a check, get a credit or debit card, and apply for a mortgage or auto or home loan.

Yet this same survey showed that *23%* of low-income Americans had no bank account. Of Americans who were paid less than $25,000 per year to begin with, almost *one in four* had no bank account.[1] This means that these individuals have no access to the goods and services that require a bank account to obtain. Even if they do manage to accumulate money, they likely feel that

---

1. Genna Contino. (2024, August 2). *23% of low-income Americans are living without a bank account.* CNBC. https://www.cnbc.com/2024/08/02/23percent-of-low-income-americans-are-living-without-a-bank-account.html

investing it or even opening a savings account is out of their reach. Taking out a business loan or home loan probably feels impossible.

This is another area where fintech can help. Thanks to digital technology and the Internet, there is no longer any reason why a person should have to physically walk into a bank in order to open a bank account. Bank accounts can be opened and deposits and transfers can be made online via smartphone.

Apps have even brought investing in buying stocks within easy reach of any individual with an Internet connection—and a bank account, which is a prerequisite for using one of the stock investing apps.

This is precisely why Novae has created services to help people find banks offering the most favorable savings account terms in their financial area, and open an account right from their computer. And there is so much more we can do to promote awareness of this service. Later in this book, we'll discuss how, with the proper legal setup, you can profit from helping unbanked people open bank accounts.

#3 Barrier to Equality: Access to Credit

Credit is a major form of financing. You might be most familiar with credit in the form of credit cards, which give you a set amount you are allowed to spend, which you might pay off each month. Loans can also be considered a form of credit, insofar as they are money which is lent to you that you are expected to pay back.

Credit is a major engine that drives the economy. It allows people to invest in building homes, businesses, and making personal choices like getting an education, that they would not otherwise have the money to do. As mentioned above, even the wealthy often use lines of credit to finance their businesses, keeping their own money safe and growing in savings and investments while starting new profit-generating operations to make them even wealthier.

Anyone is allowed to use credit in this way, but that's only possible, or a good idea, when two conditions are met. The first condition is:

1) You must have sufficient credit history, and sufficient banking access, to qualify for credit lines in the first place. Since shockingly few businesses are actually funded by the founders' out-of-pocket wealth, most people will never save up enough to build a thriving business using cash they already have. Instead, almost all successful business owners are those with good credit scores which allow them to borrow money as needed.

The biggest key to obtaining credit is credit history. This requires you to both have a bank account, and a history of successfully borrowing money and paying the loans back.

This may seem counterintuitive. If you're highly responsible and never spend money you don't have, why should you be punished for that when you finally decide to take a leap and apply for credit? But think about it this way: would you lend money to someone if you had *no* evidence that they could successfully pay it back? Would you pick someone to do a job for you that they had never done before?

Paying back borrowed money can be thought of as a job, or a

skill. Moneylenders want to see that people have experience doing it successfully before they take a big chance on someone by lending them tens of thousands of dollars. For that reason, wealthy people typically begin building their credit history as soon as they turn 18, or sometimes even earlier. They learn how to build an ideal credit history that banks will see and be very inclined to lend money to.

People who have excellent credit scores are eligible for more and larger credit lines, including business loans, home loans, credit cards, car financing, and more. And in addition to being eligible to borrow more money, they are usually offered more favorable terms; that is, lower interest rates, which means they end up paying far less on their loans in total than someone who is offered a high interest rate.

Interest rates are one of the most powerful tools in the economic toolbox. The numbers can seem small, but a difference of a few percent interest can add up to tens or hundreds of thousands of dollars owed on a business or home loan.

And, for better or worse, a lack of credit history can do far more than cut a person off from the necessary financing to create a business or buy a home. Landlords, car dealerships, retailers, and even employers are increasingly using credit scores to evaluate a person's reliability. In this day and age when credit cards and student loans are so common, having no history of paying one off may even look suspicious to landlords or employers, like you're trying to hide something. This isn't fair, but it is the truth.

The good news is, it is possible to build positive credit history surprisingly quickly by taking the right steps. And once you know what the right steps are, you can continue taking them for the rest of your life to build and maintain an excellent credit score, and you can teach your children to do the same from the moment they're eligible to have their own bank account.

This is the kind of education that wealthy families give their kids, but which I'm guessing most of you did not receive from your parents or your public schools. This is one of the invisible barriers that perpetuates economic inequality. The good news is, Novae and other financial education companies can lower this barrier to access by teaching people of all ages how to build excellent credit.

In this book we'll discuss, among other things, one of the best-kept secrets of the most successful business owners. This is the ability to build something called business credit, which allows you to separate your personal credit history from your business credit history. Building a business credit profile can make your business eligible for large amounts of financing while also protecting your personal assets.

Business credit allows you to obtain the necessary financial capacity to build your business. I've been blessed to write for platforms like Forbes.com discussing the importance of business credit and how to build it, as well as speaking on many panels at major finance conferences, and giving many talks and keynotes at small business conferences. And in Chapter 4 of this book we'll discuss how you can do this for yourself, and how fintech can help you to help *others* do it while making a profit.

This makes good business sense as well as good humanitarian sense: when our customers have access to more financing, we as a company who has a relationship with them are likely to reap some of the benefits of increased purchasing power in our customer base. This is part of what has made Novae so successful. There is also a second ingredient to prosperity through credit access that we must discuss:

2) You must have the plan and the skills to turn that credit into profit, so that you don't just end up having to pay the full amount back with interest and end up poorer than before. This is a real risk for people who borrow money without the necessary knowledge to turn it into profit.

Most new businesses fail. This can be extremely devastating if the business owner did not know how to properly plan for this likelihood. Savvy business owners know that your first business might not be the one that takes off; they also know how to conduct research to ensure that your marketing, product line, location, pricing, and other variables are correct and will support success.

The truth is, there is a science to business. There are equations you can use to predict with fairly high accuracy whether you will sell enough products to make a profit, and to improve those odds by changing different variables. Obviously, most people are not taught this science. If they were, there would be a lot more successful business owners and a lot fewer 9 to 5 employees in the world. The gatekeeping of this knowledge is another way economic inequality is perpetuated.

This is one reason I chose to make Novae a direct sales company. While this is good for me as it incentivizes my affiliates to reach new customer bases in order to make a profit for themselves, it *also* gives them a rapid education in how to build a successful business. My affiliates need to answer all the questions I mentioned above, and they receive intimate mentorship from much more experienced business owners who have a stake in their success thanks to the direct sales model.

I did not write this book to toot Novae's horn; but I *did* write it to discuss the business models that I think are best at lowering *all* barriers to wealth in a meaningful way, including the barriers created by the lack of hands-on business education most people who have not attended business school receive. Even business school itself is not a hands-on experience: it can be difficult for many students to translate what they learned in classes into actually running a successful business.

I believe that the ability to run a successful business is the path to economic freedom, and that it's important to get as many people as possible on that path in these times which are increasingly troubled by issues like wealth inequality, job loss to advancing automation and AI, and market monopolies held by megacorporations who are unscrupulous employers.

The best way I know to protect people is to teach them how to make money by working for themselves, creating their own businesses and credit histories, and how to teach others to do the same.

That's what I do at Novae, and I believe it's why we've been named one of America's fastest-growing companies four years running. We will discuss Novae's methods for helping consumers access credit, and helping aspiring people rapidly gain business and entrepreneurial expertise without student loans later in this book.

#4 Barrier to Equality: Access to Opportunity

The biggest inequality in the world is inequality of opportunity. The sad thing is that not everyone gets the same opportunities. Whether it's because of geographic location, class, your parents' income, the funding of your school district, or the color of your skin, some people will always get fewer opportunities than others.

Some people will have the opportunity to apply to business school without much stress or personal fortitude on their part being required. They will have families who are well-placed and who may even expect it of them.

I am not suggesting that these people won't work hard, but let's be realistic: they will have to work *less* hard than a student from a low-income family whose parents never went to college in order to get to the same outcome. And many students from low-income backgrounds will not make it to business school at all due to personal, family, or financial hardship, or a mere lack of role models to convince them that it is even worth applying.

I have placed inequality of opportunity fourth on this list, not because it is less important than the others, but because it is more overwhelming. Most of us have very little power to reshape school systems or other systems of power to solve this problem. But we *can* recognize the ways in which we *can* make a difference.

There are many ways to do so: run for office and vote to fund new opportunity programs for students in underserved areas. Start a business that can employ people in an underemployed area. Educate people as to how they can access opportunities that may not have been dropped in their laps.

For me, the most effective way *I* can make a difference comes back to that intersection of fintech and direct sales. By focusing on fintech, I can build products that present millions of people with financial opportunities and education that they would not have gotten through their families or schools. And by using a direct sales model, I can educate millions of people, not just in how to make money working within my business model, but in how to run *any* kind of business and obtain *any* kind of financing.

That is one of the upsides of working within the direct sales model within the fintech industry. If you make finance your business, you learn how to obtain financing for yourself, but it can work for a business or your personal life. If you make direct sales your business in an affiliate business model instead of an employee business model, you learn the skills needed to make sales *in any industry*, and to perform analyses to improve any business.

There are many ways to help create equality in our world. We need educators, politicians, and innovators across sectors who believe that equality is more important than profit.

But when I conducted my analysis of how I could help the *most* people to meet their material needs and learn the skills of financial independence, the direct sales fintech business model is what I came up with. And it may be the right answer for you, too, if you need to earn a profit, run a business, *and* empower other people all at the same time.

Throughout this book, we'll talk more about how you can get involved in the fintech direct sales business model, and obtain any training you may need from business mentors. This may be your path, or it may just be something you want academic knowledge of. But it is information that I feel deserves to be shared—if not for you, the reader, then for someone you know who is struggling to find a purpose or a career path that pays the bills.

#5 Barrier to Equality: Debt

It's no secret that debt is a major barrier to wealth inequality. In fact, too many of the world's economic systems run on debt. Increasingly, industries including medicine, housing, and education have come to rely on debt. By normalizing the practice of charging people more than they could ever afford to pay up-front, these industries have raised their prices tremendously over the last 50 years and normalized the practice of locking consumers into decades of interest-yielding debt.

Interest-yielding debt can be a very profitable asset for industries and investors of all stripes. When you know that someone is legally required to pay you every month for years to come, and that interest means they will pay you significantly more than the up-front price of your services, you can even sell their debt to others who might be willing to pay cash up-front in exchange for ownership of a debt that will yield interest over the long-term.

Unfortunately, this practice is extremely dangerous for societies in a number of ways. It reinforces inequality by incentivizing providers of essential goods and services to make services too expensive to afford up-front, since collecting debt over time is often so much more profitable. It also makes it more difficult for most people to access essential goods and services.

When the only way to obtain medical care, higher education, or housing that could create generational wealth is to go into a lifetime of debt, many people, especially those who are starting off low-income, will choose not to pursue those things at all.

When this effect becomes widespread enough in a society, societal levels of health, education, wealth, and financial security fall. Those who own the hospitals, universities, and residential properties become entitled to most of the wealth produced in the society under legal systems which allow them to charge most workers a large share of all their income. Too many people face a choice between going without, or being in debt for life.

Another form of risk is that of the debt bubble. We saw this occur during the subprime mortgage crisis of 2008, and it almost created a catastrophic domino effect that could have toppled the world economy (watch *PANIC! The Untold Story of the 2008 Financial Crisis* by HBO if you don't believe me).

In the 2008 subprime mortgage crisis, essentially, banks lent out too much money and created too much debt. The banks had reason to know that many of the debts they had created would never be paid off, and indeed, many defied government regulations in order to lend debt to people who couldn't prove that their earning capacity matched the amount of debt they were taking on. But the banks' attitude was 'we'll make this someone else's problem.'

Since they knew many of these debts would not be repaid, they *sold* the bad debts to other parties who did *not* have any reason to know that the debts were bad. These 'bad assets' made it appear that there was much more money in the global economy than there actually was, since the assets were valued on paper at the full value of the debts and loans that had been taken out, but in reality, the money to repay those debts did not exist.

I now fear we may be approaching a similar point in 2025. Medical debt, housing debt, education debt, and many other types of debt have all been treated as valuable assets. Prices have risen so high that I fear many Americans have taken out more debt than they can reasonably expect to pay back, just for survival necessities like medical care, housing, food, and education. At some point, I fear that this "bubble" will pop—the debtors, or perhaps the investors who have purchased the debt, will realize they aren't going to be paid back in full.

The consequences for the world economy when that happens is uncertain, but the consequences for consumers in the present are already clear. Growing numbers of people are choosing not to get medical care, not to buy houses, and not to go to college because these things have become so expensive. America is becoming less healthy, less educated, and more unequal.

Fortunately, the financial technology sector has the opportunity to interfere with this process in several ways. For one, we can use digital technology to help connect people to grants which might help them pay for housing, business necessities, education, and more without having to pay the money back. We can help connect people to interest-free or low-interest government loans instead of higher-interest loans from private companies.

We can also intervene in another way: through a novel model of debt relief that is growing in popularity as America's debt crisis grows.

It is a little-known fact that America's creditors often sell distressed debts for pennies on the dollar. When a creditor believes that a debt is unlikely to ever be paid, they will often sell it to an entity like a debt collector for much, much less than the full value of the original debt.

The economics of this transaction are obvious: the original creditor gets *some* money for their distressed debt, and the buyer now has the legal right to try to collect the full amount of the original debt. Often, the debt collection will be unsuccessful: the money to pay the debt simply doesn't exist. But sometimes, the debt collector will recover the full amount of the debt that is owed, and that makes the debt collecting business model quite profitable.

In recent years, though, financial businesses have been trying out a new model of debt relief. In this model, it is the consumers, not the creditor, who hires the debt assistance company to help reduce their amount of debt. The debt relief company then negotiates with the creditor to buy their debt for a much smaller amount than the original amount owed—and splits the difference with the debtor, resulting in a significantly smaller total payoff amount.

Debt relief companies in this business do have to profit, so they must charge debtors more than the amount they buy the debt for. But because they have the customer's willing participation, they are able to charge much less than the full debt amount typically demanded by traditional debt collectors while still turning a profit and helping people to reduce their overall debt load significantly.

We will discuss how you can profit *and* help people using this business model later in this book.

Now that you've had a small taste of the societal dangers of financial inequality and its causes, perhaps you can see how fintech has the possibility to transform America's economic landscape. And perhaps you can see why I've chosen the direct sales model for my own fintech company as the one which allows me to make the biggest difference for the largest number of people.

In the chapters to come, we'll investigate each of these major barriers to equality, and the ways in which fintech can dismantle them while *also* profiting its entrepreneurs and sales professionals, in more detail.

We'll see how we can create a kinder, more equal world together, without having to sacrifice our ambitions for wealth and fortune.

Chapter 2
The Rise of Fintech

The word "fintech" is a combination of the words "financial" and "technology." It refers to the application of technology to finance. This does include technologies as "old school" as the first use of the telegraph and telephone to authorize financial transactions.

While they hardly feel cutting-edge, these examples give you some idea of the revolutionary power of fintech. After all, before the telegraph and telephone, financial transactions could *only* be conducted in-person or via snail mail. Trades and purchases between people who weren't standing face-to-face in the same city took weeks or months, with "months" being the rule for transactions that required the crossing of an ocean.

Back in those days, only people who could already afford to buy large amounts of physical goods, factories, and land could become entrepreneurs. You had to own a physical means of production to have any financial independence, and since laws were made by the ruling classes, the means of creating and owning wealth stayed almost entirely with the ruling classes.

One reason the American frontier was revolutionary for Europeans was that, after European diseases had killed many indigenous people, there was a lot of land which ordinary people could claim and use to grow food or mine minerals, which they could turn into wealth. This was *not* the case in Europe, where virtually all land was already owned by wealthy nobles who basically also owned the people who worked the land.

This might be one reason why America has been such a hotbed of entrepreneurship for the last few centuries: Europeans were accustomed to a world where almost all assets were owned by the ruling class, and ordinary people had little to no opportunity to build wealth for themselves. Americans, on the other hand, spent centuries in a situation where hard work could make a person fabulously wealthy.

Now that so many assets are digital and not reliant on physical means of production, we are in such an era again. Financial technology is a new frontier rich with opportunities. And since it is actually being created by us, not just "discovered," we don't even have to kick anybody off the land in order to claim some for ourselves. In fact, this is one frontier where we can profit by helping others get set up with their own piece of financial real estate.

Since the rise of the telegraph and telephone, financial technology has grown at an exponential rate. Electronics turned the stock market from a physical place where papers were traded into a global marketplace that anyone could participate in almost in real time.

Credit cards, introduced in the mid-20th century, were the first method that allowed people to pay by directly connecting to an account instead of using cash or checks.

The rise of the Internet in the late 20th century saw the beginning of the current fintech revolution. Banks figured out pretty quickly that the Internet would allow customers to access their bank accounts remotely, allowing real-time withdrawals, deposits, and balance transfers from any home or business computer.

The emergence of online trading platforms like E*TRADE soon followed, with online stock trading making investing more accessible to the general public. Before, special knowledge and access had been required to trade on the stock market. Now, anyone who had a computer could do it.

As technology improved and computers became steadily smaller and more affordable, "anyone with a computer" stopped meaning "elite people who had money" and came to mean "literally anyone who had access to a smartphone or a public library."

During the Dot-Com Boom and Bust of the 1990s, billions of dollars were poured into new online companies who were competing for the massive wild west that was online real estate. While most failed, a number of online financial services platforms such as PayPal were alongside Amazon and Google as companies that emerged successful and changed the way we live entirely.

In the 21st century, the offspring of these successful models have been proliferating, making banking and financial services more accessible than ever before.

Online banking has now completely eliminated the need for

physical bank branches for many people. More payment platforms like Zelle and Venmo have adapted PayPal's model, with competition between the apps fueling lower transfer fees and faster transaction processing. Other tech companies like Google and Apple have introduced their own Pay programs, allowing you to route money through them as part of their technological ecosystem.

Apps like Robinhood have led to the rise of "the retail investor"—investors who are not wealthy power players, but who invest their spare money as a hobby or side hustle, and who make up for their relatively small individual purchasing power with their millions-strong population. This has combined with the rise of "cryptocurrencies" to make and break fortunes by moving trillions of dollars in and out of virtual currencies that aren't regulated by any government.

The promise of "decentralized finance," in which currency supply and value is controlled by users as a collective, rather than a central governing body, has proven to be a very sharp double-edged sword.

Quite a few "crypto millionaires" have preached about the virtues of a currency which is free from taxation and government interference, while many others have found themselves tens of thousands of dollars in debt due to wild market fluctuations. Analysts have worried about what the loss of value from taxable currencies could do to funding for public services.

Financial products like insurance also went virtual, with almost any type of insurance now being purchasable by the push of a button on your smartphone. This has made insurance much more accessible, with millions more people now insured against disaster due to the accessibility while insurance companies make record profits from the new customers.

Most recently, starting in 2018 the rise of open banking APIs (Application Programming Interfaces) have led to a renewed explosion in financial and banking products being offered virtually. This technology has allowed innovators to more easily build on the infrastructure of existing banks and financial institutions, leading to an explosion of new products and competition.

Some of these developments fight inequality and build financial security by offering ease of access to banking and financial products. Others are dangerous: in many cases these direct-to-consumer processes bypass government regulations and financial advisors, leaving people vulnerable to losing wealth as easily as they can make it by investing in volatile stocks or predatory financial products.

This is the chaotic, promising yet perilous milieu we find ourselves in today. In many ways, the current digital landscape bears a strong resemblance to the Wild West. Almost anything is possible, for better or worse. Relatively few laws exist governing these new inventions, laws that do exist often go unenforced, and treasure troves of new possibility are waiting to be discovered like the untapped gold veins of the Wild West.

Just like in the Wild West, a person who is well-informed, prepared to defend themselves from predators, and take advantage of the new territory waiting to be claimed can make a fortune. But a person who is not well-informed is vulnerable to being taken advantage of, or even becoming a casualty in the territory wars between the rising powers of the Information Age economy.

With this book, I hope to arm you with knowledge. We'll discuss what I believe to be some of the most promising untapped gold veins in the fintech landscape, as well as red flags to look for to avoid being taken advantage of by unscrupulous players.

Let's talk some more about the most important principles and services in fintech, so you can know what opportunities lie waiting to be mined, and what principles you must use to mine them successfully.

#1 Customer Centricity

Competition among fintech products and services is fierce. Because almost anyone can design a new service or build a new piece of software, those which give customers the best experience in every way emerge triumphant. Even something as simple as a confusing interface can make the difference between success or failure in fintech.

Some common ways of succeeding in the arena of user experience include:

1. User-friendly interfaces. The interface should be intuitive, simple, easy to navigate, and it must *work* without glitches. Interfaces that don't make it clear how to operate the app, confuse the user with too much text or too many options, or frequently glitch and fail are likely to drive

users away.

2. Personalized experiences. Often the best deals a customer can get are personalized for their specific circumstances. Fintech providers that can offer services tailored to an individual's specific needs and preferences will pull ahead of the pack in competition.

3. 24/7 access. People don't usually tolerate websites that don't work 24/7, and the same is true of any fintech software or website. Fintech products must work 24/7 or users will flee to the competition.

4. Pro-active customer support. This area is a powerful opportunity to distinguish yourself, since even some giant players in the fintech field struggle to excel here. Websites and applications that have highly knowledgeable, rapidly responsive customer service provide a great user experience for customers when confusion strikes or something doesn't work properly.

Even tech giants like Meta, Amazon, and PayPal have often been criticized for having customer service that is difficult to reach, slow to respond, and often unhelpful. If you can beat them on customer service, people may decide they'd rather work with you.

Take a moment to think about the fintech products you use,

such as payment applications, online banking portals, and online insurance portals. Can you think of areas where they could improve on one or more of these parameters?

Now ask yourself: does this area of improvement represent a potential business opportunity for you as a competitor or service provider? If your answer is "yes," we'll discuss how to learn the business and get your fintech venture funded using business credit later in this book. Here are some of the top products where we can see the principles of customer centricity at play:

- Mobile banking apps. There are two main reasons these are so popular. One is that people really, really want to be able to bank remotely. The more they can do in terms of financial transactions from the comfort of their smart phone, the more convenient and efficient their lives.

  The other reason comes from existing banks. Market research shows that customers are more likely to buy from a company if they regularly enter the product's online ecosystem. This is why almost all businesses, even those like coffee shops and restaurants, have been developing their own apps recently.

  By having their own app, any business can offer loyalty programs like reward points, special discounts, and send customers personalized ads and coupons. People then spent more money with the business and are more likely to return to the business instead of going to the competition.

- Personalized financial advice. AI-powered tools can now give advice for everything from credit repair and debt relief to investment guidance. If you can build an AI that can give this type of advice and help to consumers, or find a way to contract or profit off of one that already exists, you can start a business that profits by helping people with financial matters.

We'll discuss more about some AI-powered tools and opportunities for you to profit by licensing existing financial technology later in this book.

- Customer service chatbots. Although many customers complain about these chatbots being impersonal and ineffective at answering specialized questions, these chatbots are designed to meet customers' needs for highly responsive 24/7 support. By gleaning answers to common questions from databases, these chatbots can help customers with many common questions no matter what the date or time.

#2 *Innovation and Technology*

Those fintech companies which are most wildly successful are those who have accomplished one of two things:

1. Meeting a new need that no one had previously seen or attempted to meet, such as PayPal and Google, or

2. Leveraging advancing technology to meet a well-known need better than ever before, such as Amazon.

Some common key areas where technology has been used to enhance finance in recent decades include:

- Improving efficiency by streamlining processes and reducing operational costs. The automation of using algorithms, software programs, and AIs to perform data processing tasks that would once have needed to be done manually is an excellent example of this that applies to almost all modern highly successful fintech products.

    It also applies to companies like Amazon, Chewy, and other online-based retailers that have used new technologies in combination with innovative thinking to create unrivaled customer experiences in highly cost-effective ways.

- Developing new products. Companies that create innovative solutions for new or unmet customer needs are also likely to be highly successful. This was PayPal back when the dawn of online retail created demand for a way to pay for goods electronically.

This also applies to physical product companies like meal delivery kits and meal delivery services, which were almost nonexistent during the COVID-19 pandemic, but became extremely popular as lockdown closed both grocery stores and restaurants. Now, customers are hooked on the convenience.

- Enhancing security. In a world where more and more currency is digital, the incentive to hack financial accounts is growing by the minute. As such, technologies that protect customer data and prevent fraud are a necessity, and a lucrative one for those who can find innovative ways to prevent hacks.

The skyrocketing popularity of services like Virtual Private Networks to protect data in recent years testifies to how an old technology can be brought to a new use to address new needs, and behind-the-scenes companies like Crowdstrike routinely close multimillion dollar deals with companies by offering innovative security solutions.

Let's take a look at some services that have offered totally new innovations in the fields of security and efficiency:

- Blockchain technology enables secure and transparent

transactions in areas like cryptocurrency and lending. While the claim to be uncrackable is a bold one, so far this technology seems to be the closest thing we have to an impenetrable barrier against the theft or malicious editing of digital information. This is one reason many people believe it will be the basis for future currencies.

- Artificial intelligence (AI) and machine learning allow computers to perform more complex and nuanced operations than ever before at extremely high speeds. In the finance world, AI has been used to improve fraud detection, yield more reliable credit scores, and offer more personalized financial advice and recommendations to customers.

- Cloud computing provides scalable and cost-effective infrastructure for fintech operations. By decentralizing computing power, security against hardware failures is enhanced and the hardware used to make complex calculations does not necessarily have to be kept on-site, or even owned by the company doing the calculations.

#3 Financial Inclusion

Fintech has the ability to make financial services accessible to everyone, including underserved populations. Because it removes many geographical and logistical barriers to accessing and delivering financial services, it opens the doors to finance to groups including:

- The unbanked and underbanked: Individuals without access to traditional banking services. Whether living in an inner-city neighborhood with no bank branches or a small town that has just one, individuals who have no or limited access to physical banks can now access almost any financial service imaginable through remote banking and other financial technologies.

- Those who have historically faced discrimination. Whether due to education level, culture, race, or disability, traditional banks have often discriminated against those who they believe will not have the ability to pay back loans or make big investments for questionable reasons. When financial decisions are automated or take place without a face-to-face meeting, much of the potential for discrimination disappears.

Let's take a look at some fintech services that break down geographic and socioeconomic barriers to make banking, financing, and financial education accessible to everyone:

- Mobile money transfers enable convenient and affordable money transfers to remote areas. The importance of this in a global economy where the availability of money has historically been based on the residents' ability to sell physical goods at market cannot be overstated.

- Microloans and microfinance provide small loans to entrepreneurs and individuals with limited credit history. Again, the importance cannot be overstated: in underserved areas, the ability to start a successful business or learn a lucrative skill can come down to just a few hundred or thousand dollars.

Such microfunding has historically been unavailable thanks to institutional focus on large transactions and reluctance to lend to people who were not already wealthy.

- Financial literacy programs educate individuals on financial concepts and responsible money management. While much of this knowledge was traditionally gatekept to upper-class families and institutions of higher education, the Information Age makes it accessible to anyone online for little to no cost. This is transformative for reasons we will discuss throughout this book.

#4 Data Security and Privacy

Protecting customer data is paramount, not just for ethical reasons, but for reasons of self-preservation. Fintech companies are some of the most appealing targets for hackers since they deal directly with financial accounts and data. Failure to protect these accounts and computer systems can result in serious harm to customers—and guarantee that no one ever trusts the company with their money again.

For that reason, fintech companies must implement robust security measures. To remain safe, they must employ encryption, multi-factor authentication, and fraud detection systems. They must also comply with data privacy regulations such as those spelled out by the European Union's General Data Protection Regulations and California Consumer Privacy Act.

These regulations often require companies to be transparent with customers. In addition to keeping data safe from hackers, fintech companies must comply with the law about who they intentionally sell customer data to. Several scandals in recent years have led to loss of public confidence in companies that were found to be selling customer data to third parties like advertisers and AI training companies without customers' knowledge.

Companies which engage in such practices of non-consensual customer data selling and sharing may find themselves entirely legally unable to operate in a state, country, or even the entire European Union if they do not comply with regulations about transparency.

New transparency regulations can also be passed at any time, and may result in a company being unable to operate in that area if they are not already operating above and beyond the standards required by existing laws.

Let's take a look at some services that use advancing technology to offer cutting-edge data security:

- Biometric authentication utilizes fingerprint or facial recognition for secure login. In theory, this allows only a specific individual to access an account or device. Any attacker would at least need the necessary information about the customer's biometrics to be able to attempt to duplicate them.

- Fraud monitoring and alert systems proactively detecting and preventing fraudulent activities. While those texts you occasionally get asking if a bank transaction was really made by you, complex algorithms that determine whether purchases are within your usual pattern of financial behavior can save you much bigger headaches by quickly recognizing if your information has been stolen.

- Data encryption protects sensitive customer information through advanced encoding techniques. Encryption is part of a data arms race, with hackers constantly working to develop more powerful methods to crack encryptions. This means that data security firms must constantly have equally motivated teams working on developing better encryption methods.

#5 *Regulatory Compliance*

Fintech companies must operate within a legal and regulatory framework. In fact, if they wish to operate in all 50 US states and/or globally, they often most comply with *multiple* regulatory frameworks where laws and regulations are different in different geographic areas. This is why regulatory compliance is often an entire department within technology companies, and a prime target for AI automation.

Common types of regulations tech companies must adhere to include:

- Data security and privacy regulations, like discussed under the previous bullet point.

- Financial regulations such as Anti-Money Laundering (AML) regulations) and Know-Your-Customer (KYC) regulations that guarantee that the holders of financial accounts are real individuals and not aliases or shell corporations.

- Building trust and credibility. Companies that demonstrate a commitment to ethical and responsible business practices, even above and beyond the requirements of the law, often build a loyal following and may have a competitive edge over less scrupulous providers. Trust that a company will do the right thing even when no one is watching is a key part of consumer decision-making processes.

Let's look at some services which use advancing technology to help corporations remain compliant with necessary laws and regulations, as well as ethical principles.

- KYC and AML compliance solutions help businesses verify customer identities. Because the software knows what the legal requirements for identity verification are, the company does not have to manually review the requirements each time a new customer's identity is verified.

- Regulatory reporting tools can help companies to automatically gather necessary data and report it to compliance agencies. Whether the process is fully automated or overseen by a human, these software programs can vastly reduce the time and energy involved in ensuring compliance while still improving results.

Now that you've gotten a taste of the history and capabilities of financial technology, let's examine how fintech can be used to reduce inequality and profit you, both as a customer and potentially as service provider and business owner.

Chapter 3

How Fintech Equalizes Access to Capital

Capital is the engine that drives capitalism. These days the term "capital" is typically used as a shorthand for "money," but its dictionary definition offers us deeper insight into why capital is so important and powerful. According to Investopedia:

"Capital is a broad term that can describe anything that confers value or benefit to its owners, such as a factory and its machinery, intellectual property like patents, or the financial assets of a business or an individual."[1]

This is why you'll sometimes also hear people refer to things like

---

1. Hargrave, M. (n.d.). Capital: Definition, how it's used, structure, and types in business. Investopedia. https://www.investopedia.com/terms/c/capital.asp

"social capital" (the amount of influence you have socially), or similar terms. Capital is often discussed in terms of dollar amounts, because in our society money is the unit we use to measure value. But in reality, capital is nothing more or less than the ability to *create* value. Money, machines, property, and ideas are all forms of capital that can be converted into wealth.

This is important because it gives us a hint at one cause of economic inequality. Arguably the most reliable way to create wealth is to already *have* capital. It is typically those who are already wealthy who can afford to buy properties that will gain value in the coming years, machines and factories, or pay software development teams and marketing teams, to turn their ideas into products that can be mass produced and sold, making large amounts of profit.

This perpetuates inequality by ensuring that it is much easier for people born rich to become even richer than for people who were *not* born rich to turn their ideas and labor into assets that gain value over time.

People who cannot afford to own homes or start businesses are forced to spend their money renting from others while gaining no wealth from property ownership; people who cannot afford to start businesses are forced to spend their lives working for employers who keep most of the value of the employees' labor for themselves.

Meanwhile, people who started out wealthy in the first place are able to buy property and start businesses which make them wealthier and wealthier over time, and which create wealth that can be passed on to their children.

This, in fact, is why Karl Marx was of the opinion that capitalism inherently creates and perpetuates inequality: those who owned the means of production, like factories (software development teams hadn't been invented in his time) would always be able to gain more wealth by profiting off of the labor of employees, while average workers would be unlikely to amass enough wealth to buy a factory of their own and start their own business.

However, modern financial systems have changed that in one crucial way. Today, businesses are often started and homes purchased, not with the wealth a person *already* has, but with capital acquired through bank loans and other forms of credit lines. This means that a person doesn't have to start out wealthy to acquire property, machines, or other forms of capital that can create huge amounts of wealth.

There is still a component of inequality in this system, because, as we discussed in Chapter 1, it is the people who are already wealthy who are most likely to be able to secure capital to borrow. This is due to a combination of education and financial history.

Children of wealthy families are likely taught how to obtain loans and build a business by their parents, and grow up believing this is a realistic thing for them to do. Children of wealthy families are also likely to begin building positive credit history at an early age, without any of the damage to their credit history that can occur as a result of poverty or lack of education about credit scores and their importance.

Other barriers to obtaining home and business loans have historically been geography and discrimination. If you live in a neighborhood with few or no bank branches, it is harder to obtain a bank account, much less impress a loan officer in an in-person meeting whose results will determine whether your loan is approved.

Historically, the practices of in-person banking followed by decisions made by human loan officers made it very easy for discrimination to bar people from capital. Those who were deemed to be too poor, lacking in formal education, or of the wrong race, gender, or culture by loan officers could be denied loans even if the official reason given for the denial was something different.

However, these barriers to equality are beginning to fall away, one layer at a time, due to advancing technology. First, the very concept of home loans and business loans as common practices made it possible for people who weren't born wealthy to acquire enough capital to buy a home or start a business.

Now, the shift to digital banking is removing the requirements for in-person banking and reducing the influence of discrimination in lending decisions. In fact, many lending decisions are now made by computer algorithms that assess a person's financial history, but which are less likely than human loan officers to suffer from subconscious biases based on a borrower's home neighborhood, level of formal education, race, gender, or other elements that can perpetuate inequality.

Let's briefly examine in more detail what are, in my opinion, the two most important forms of capital for building generational wealth that you can pass on to your children and grandchildren.

Home Ownership and Generational Wealth

"Generational wealth" refers to wealth that changes not just your own life, but the future of your family for generations to come. It typically takes the form of large assets such as properties or businesses which are valued at $100,000 or more, and which can be sold or otherwise leveraged by your descendants to create an ongoing source of income or a large amount of wealth.

Homeownership is one of the most common forms of generational wealth. Everyone lives somewhere, and that really goes one of two ways. Either you rent your living space, meaning you pay a lot of money to a landlord and get no long-term value in return; or you own your home, and the mortgage payments you make stay with you forever in the form of equity of your home.

Many people don't even fully realize this dichotomy. Homeowners and renters often have similar housing expenses, but in the case of renters that expense goes into the pocket of a landlord and is never seen by the tenant again. For homeowners, those payments are payments on a property they *own*, which will stay in their family until they decide to sell it or rent it to tenants as a lucrative form of passive income.

The value of homeownership cannot be overstated. In the last 20 years, for example, the values of many U.S. residential properties have roughly doubled; this means that people who bought homes 20 years ago can now sell them for twice what they paid, or rent them to create a generous passive income. In one case, a family I know bought their home in the early 2000s for $225,000; in 2022, they sold it for $450,000.

Now, you might ask, "How are we supposed to pay $225,000 for a home in the first place if we're not wealthy?" And this is where fintech's ability to lower barriers to wealth comes in. Most people only pay a relatively small fraction of the cost of their home as a down payment, paying off the vast majority of the cost through mortgage payments over time.

Mortgages are one form of borrowing capital. You are essentially "borrowing" your house from the bank until you have paid off your mortgage in full, at which point you are the full owner of the home and you and your family will not owe any further money for housing as long as it remains in your possession.

This means that mortgages are one point where financial education and discrimination can become barriers to wealth.

People with poor credit scores are most likely denied mortgages, or may be offered mortgages with very high interest rates that verge on the predatory. Just a few percentage points in the interest rate on a large loan such as a mortgage can mean that a person with a low credit score may pay *over $100,000 more* for the same home as a person with an excellent credit score. Let's do the math on that.

Suppose you are applying for a $400,000 30-year mortgage. This means that you'll pay off the $400,000 mortgage over the course of 30 years—but you'll also pay interest, which means you will pay extra money *on top of* the $400,000 you originally borrowed to pay for your home. That interest accumulates over time, so when applying an interest rate to a large sum over the course of 30 years you can end up being charged a *lot* of interest.

Let's say that the same mortgage is offered to two different people with two different terms. For people with excellent credit scores who the banks know will make timely payments, the interest rate charged may be as low as 6.9% based on today's lending environment in 2025; for someone with a poor credit score, they may be denied a mortgage entirely *or* may be charged rates as high as 8.6%. Let's see how that 1.7% different plays out when paying off a $400,000 house over the course of 30 years:

Total payoff amount for paying back $400,000.00 at 6.9% interest over 30 years: $948,384. Interest paid: $584,384.

Total payoff amount for paying back $400,000 at 8.6% interest over 30 years: $1,117,456. Interest paid: $717,456.

As you can see, these are still some pretty intimidating numbers. It can be easy for people to feel that home ownership, and therefore generational wealth for their family, is not realistic for them. That is why it is more important now than ever that we act to increase our own wealth. Using the tools we discuss in this book will help you to do this; going into business with an opportunity in fintech will help you even more.

We will discuss some business opportunities in fintech that are available in later chapters. For now, let's continue to learn about barriers to equality and different ways that fintech can help lower them, whether you are engaging with it as a fintech professional or business owner, or as a consumer.

The cost of a down payment on a home can also be prohibitive. Even if one is "only" paying 10% of the value of your home in a down payment, that can still come to $20,000-$50,000 required up front, which is an amount of money that most families work for years or even decades to save. Fortunately, this is another area where fintech can help.

Programs exist to help people with the down payments for their homes, especially if they have low incomes, or people who aspire to be first-generation homeowners. The federal government administers special grants and mortgages to help people in these situations, as do some state governments, city governments, and private institutions.

Fintech can make it easier than ever before to find and access these grants, now that most are advertised online. Simply knowing that a resource exists is half the battle: figuring out how to access it and taking the necessary steps to do so is the other half.

All of those steps are made much easier by digital technology which allows anyone to search for grants and loans they may qualify for, and especially by fintech companies which may provide searchable databases and assistance in applying for these programs. The service I've assembled, NovaeGrants.com, for example, is a free search platform that gives business owners a list of grants they might qualify for.

Remember, a grant is not a loan: it is free money designed to support certain types of economic activity, which does not need to be paid back. All you need to do is prove to the grant funding agency that you will be effective at accomplishing the economic or community service goal they support.

This is an excellent example of an opportunity to profit in fintech. Fintech business owners may be able to profit from helping people access these opportunities, but how much greater is the profit for their customer if the customer successfully obtains a grant which enables them to buy a home worth hundreds of thousands of dollars?

This is why fintech is such a rapidly growing field: when done properly, your customers end up with *more* money, not less. This is obviously very good for creating referral networks and repeat business.

One last topic we need to discuss under the umbrella of home ownership as generational wealth is the business model of property ownership.

It's no secret that landlords can become very wealthy. If living space is an expensive and necessary commodity, a great deal of passive income can come from renting out a room, a home, or an entire apartment complex that you own. For this reason, some people who are serious about creating generational wealth for their families are focusing on buying up property, not just as a place to live, but as a business proposition.

I will be transparent: I am not a big fan of huge, corporate landlords who buy up huge swaths of property, removing the ability of families to purchase the properties and become wealthy themselves. But even having a single extra property which you rent to tenants can be a profound source of financial security, creating ongoing mostly-passive income in the form of rent payments.

This kind of small landlord renting can also perform a profound service to your tenants. As an ethical landlord with only a small number of rental properties, you can offer affordable living space to people who may not be able or willing to buy their own homes at this time.

Many young people wait to buy homes until later in life because they wish to have the freedom to move around, or because they don't wish to be locked into a mortgage payment. Other families may be simply unable to buy their own home due to a necessity to build up their credit or funding for a down payment. For those people, having an ethical family landlord who charges affordable rent and actually cares about the welfare of their tenants can be a huge blessing.

For these reasons, ownership of a second property is an option worth considering when you are looking to build generational wealth for your family and provide affordable living space for others in your community at the same time. And this is an excellent segue into another major way of building generational wealth: business ownership.

Business Ownership and Generational Wealth

Home ownership is a common but limited form of generational wealth. Although it can seem daunting, anyone can own a home with the proper application of financial knowledge, strategy, and hard work. Home ownership makes sense for nearly everyone as a financial strategy because it means owning an extremely valuable asset whose value is only likely to increase over time.

However, home ownership is not the only, or even the most powerful, way to build generational wealth. I own a home; I also own a business. In an ideal scenario, business ownership is the key to ultimate freedom. It means working for yourself and keeping all the profits of your labor (which employees working for other people don't get to do). Depending on the type of business you choose, it could also mean freedom to travel, make your own hours, and more.

This does not mean that business ownership is *easy*. Becoming a CEO will be the most difficult thing you ever do. But that isn't a bad thing.

There is a misconception that comfort and convenience are what make us happy. In reality, psychological research shows that happiness is a reward mechanism in the brain. It is not merely an absence of pain or hardship: it is a reward our brain gives us when we do something right. Happiness is what we experience when we make a loved one smile, or accomplish a difficult task. That is why difficult tasks are often described as "rewarding."

Running a business isn't for everyone. To successfully support oneself as a business owner involves taking on a tremendous amount of responsibility and working harder than you have ever worked in your life. For a while.

But once you have learned the necessary skills to run a business—another thing most schools don't teach you how to do, and even MBA programs generally won't give you the hands-on experience you need to really learn what works in the business world—you will have an incredible amount of power in your hands. You will have the power to create wealth, employment opportunities, and valuable services from scratch.

I recommend this learning experience to almost everyone in the modern economy, because it is the best way not to be at the mercy of the job market or of fluctuating wages. Most employees get relatively few opportunities to negotiate to increase their pay; business owners can increase their revenue, and their profits, at any time by learning more, innovating, and changing their business model. This is not *easy*, but it is a form of power that only business owners have.

Businesses create wealth for their owners by creating value for customers. When a business successfully delivers things people want to pay for consistently, it becomes a reliable source of wealth. This means that as long as its owners can successfully manage to adapt the business to changing market conditions, they have a guaranteed source of income. No one is going to fire the owner.

Business owners can even sell their businesses to new owners at a massive profit. When someone "buys out" a business, it means that they have purchased the business from the owner. And because the purchase price must outweigh the money the business owner would have made from the business if they had *not* sold it, even relatively small businesses often sell for millions of dollars. The buyer is buying all of the business's potential to make money in the future.

So whether you wish to get your children into the family business and pass along the generational wealth that way, or you wish to sell your business upon your retirement and use your wealth to help your children buy their own homes and start their own businesses, business ownership is the best source of generational wealth there is.

This is because, unlike with home ownership, a business can grow and scale. The value of property will always be constrained by the attributes of that property. A piece of property can't experience unlimited growth; in fact, property owners can't directly control the value of their property in any way. They don't have control over the environment in which their property is situated, which will limit the value of their property and may adversely affect it.

The size and value of a business, on the other hand, is only limited by its owners' motivation and imagination. At least, that's the case once the owner has acquired the financial knowledge to be able to create and execute financial strategies successfully.

Obviously, few people have tens of thousands of dollars with which to start and scale a business lying around. But once a person becomes learned and practiced in how to access capital, the ability to access capital is limited only by the business owner's ability to turn capital into profit. As long as a business owner can successfully convert business loans and other forms of capital into profit, there is no limit to how large or profitable their business can become.

Business ownership can mean many things. Every online shop and corner store is a business. A podcast or YouTube channel can be a business as well.

Some businesses are run for reasons of passion: a person just really wants to do something with their life, so they start a business in that craft or industry, even if it's not the easiest or most profitable type of business to run. Other businesses are run for financial reasons: a person wants to build generational wealth for themselves or their families, so they choose a business model that optimizes their ability to do that.

I am of the opinion that businesses can be run for both passion *and* profit. With sufficient ingenuity, almost any passion can be turned into a profitable business model. And it is my opinion that, in the fintech space, the most profitable business models can also feed the passion most of us innately have for helping and uplifting others.

When creating a business for the purposes of creating generational wealth, there are a few characteristics you want to make sure your business model has:

1. Scalability. I am putting this first because, in my opinion, it is the single biggest cause of struggle and hardship among business owners. All business owners think about how to monetize their craft; few think about how they can continue growing the value of their business; serving more and more customers with each passing year.

   It is scalability which allows a business to become wildly valuable in a way that can sustain your family's financial independence for generations to come.

2. Agility. We live in rapidly changing times. Most of the businesses that I've seen fail have failed because they failed to adapt their products and services, or their marketing and distribution strategy, to keep up with the times. Think of all the big box retail giants that went out of business because they could not compete with the rise of digital shopping.

I am of the opinion that almost any type of business can be made agile; but you as the business owner have to *be* agile. When your business is in trouble, you must respond by figuring out how to change your products, services, distribution, and/or marketing to improve the situation. This is a mindset.

I believe that the field of fintech is an ideal field in terms of scalability and agility.

Because its products are mostly digital, they can easily be scaled to deliver to millions or even billions of people if they are products and services that millions or billions of people *want* to purchase. The fact that fintech products often actually leave their customers with more money than they started with can also be considered an aspect of scalability. When done right, the products and services you deliver constantly increase the future purchasing power of your customer base.

Because there are so many rich pieces of knowledge and opportunities that can enrich people in the field of finance, and because advancing technology creates almost limitless potential ways to package and deliver that information and those opportunities, fintech is an incredibly versatile field which an agile CEO can easily adapt to almost any change in market conditions.

I believe that any industry or business model can become scalable and agile with sufficient ingenuity. The main things that are required are access to information, and a mindset of radical responsibility. Luckily for us, this is the Information Age; anyone with an Internet connection can learn how to do almost anything.

The "radical responsibility" bit is harder. It means that we must take personal responsibility for everything that happens in or to our business. At first, this can seem unrealistic or unfair to many people; how can we be responsible for market conditions?

But here is the key: anything we are responsible for, we can change. You can't control market conditions, but you can take responsibility for finding new products, services, and methods of distribution and marketing that *will* work under current market conditions. This is what I mean when I say growth is limited only by your imagination.

If you don't do that, your business will fail. But if you *do* take radical responsibility for all the steps necessary to succeed, your ability to build wealth is limitless.

How Fintech Can Help

Based on the descriptions above, you probably have some idea of several ways in which fintech can help anyone to access capital and subsequently build generational wealth. To put these benefits in the form of a neat list, properly utilized fintech can:

1. Teach people how to build great credit histories, which will give them access to better mortgages and business loans, and subsequently to potentially unlimited financing for generational wealth for their family.

2. Educate people about, and connect them to, options such as grants, government programs, and low-interest loans which are specifically designed to be more accessible to people who are struggling to raise the down payment on a house.

3. Teach people what they need to know to become successful business owners by connecting them to business education, mentorship, and opportunities to actually go into business in fintech.

My company Novae, for example, has built its affiliate program specifically to allow people to begin running their own fintech businesses with mentorship and resources from my company, even if they have no higher education or previous business experience. Many of our top-performing affiliates entered the direct sales industry with no prior higher education or experience.

> The expertise learned on the job and through mentorship in the direct sales industry is, in my opinion, among the best business education options on the planet.

I wanted to open with this discussion of capital, because capital and its power and distribution are at the heart of the rest of this book, and indeed at the heart of our very world economy. Practically speaking, our world today runs on capital: even countries which are communist in name are, in practice, moved by money and capital.

Whether we like it or not, this is the world we live in. We cannot escape the necessity to make money—so our best power move to protect ourselves and our loved ones and gain influence on the world is to instead master the art of making it.

Throughout the rest of this book, we will discuss in more detail how fintech can reduce economic inequality by making financial literacy, excellent credit scores, access to opportunity, and debt reduction accessible to anyone with an Internet connection.

We'll also see how you can become very wealthy by entering this industry while feeling great about helping millions of people. No college degree or expensive startup costs required.

Chapter 4

How Fintech Can Improve Financial Education

"Financial education" is a term that is often misunderstood. Too many people have sold this term as being all about budgeting, but it is so much more than that. As we've already discussed, how you interact with the financial system is much more than just what you do or don't spend money on. Financial education means learning:

- How money moves in the national and global economies.

- How homes and businesses are financed.

- How interest rates can make you very poor or very rich, depending on what financial activities you engage in.

- The difference between a predatory credit line and a helpful credit line, and how to make sure you're getting the good ones.

- How banks determine a person's creditworthiness, both in terms of personal and business credit (they're slightly different from each other).

- How you can make yourself someone banks *want* to lend money to.

- And much more.

The saying that "you can't save your way out of poverty" is quite true. Obtaining wealth *does* require saving some money, but saving money alone is not nearly enough. Instead, it is necessary to know how to use the money you've saved to obtain much, much more money. This is the knowledge that financial education can impart.

This might all sound a bit intimidating, and rightly so. If it were easy and simple to learn how finance works in detail, many more people would be successful business owners. But think of it like this: finance is a game. It's like learning a sport or strategy game with very complex rules. If you can learn the rules, stats, and strategies of football, basketball, chess, or Warhammer (the most popular strategy game of 2024, I'm told) you can learn to successfully execute financial strategies that create wealth.

Basics of Financial Education

There won't be room to teach you everything there is to know about financial education in this book. But for your knowledge, major opportunities to either learn or start a business teaching in financial education include:

#1 Budgeting

The most basic aspect of financial education is, indeed, budgeting. Budgeting is simply the idea of planning how much you will spend throughout the week, month, or year, and sticking to that plan.

Many people learn budgeting early as their adult years, as it is often necessary to survive when receiving an entry-level paycheck. But those who are introduced to credit cards early in life may *not* learn budgeting, as they may use credit cards to cover expenses their paychecks don't cover. This can result in a situation where people spend their lives in debt to banks.

This is, of course, exactly what banks want: they *want* you to owe them interest payments for the rest of your life. We've already seen just how much money a seemingly low interest payment can add up to in the previous chapter.

There are times when it makes sense to charge things on credit cards as part of a financial strategy. For example, I charge almost everything to credit cards with low interest rates and high limits before paying all my credit cards off in full each month. This profits me because I have executed a strategy to obtain low-interest, high-limit cards where I will pay very little to no interest and my credit score will not suffer as a result of charging thousands of dollars each month.

This strategy allows me to accrue large amounts of credit card rewards which can be used to purchase things for my home or business, but mostly free travel. My family and I take a couple international vacations each year paid for by points from credit rewards.

Because my card limits are high, I build positive credit history by charging thousands of dollars per month and paying it all off in full, instead of harming my credit history by charging too much relative to my credit limit.

I give the banks no opportunity to charge me interest, but the rewards programs give me extra value and increase my wealth beyond what I would have had by buying everything using cash in the first place. This is an example of the power of financial education and financial strategy. Because I understand exactly how budgeting, credit scores, and credit lines work, I am able to profit off of using credit cards.

If I did not know how to budget so I could pay off my cards in full every month, or if I had not put in the strategy and work to obtain low-interest, high-limit credit cards and select good rewards programs in the first place, charging my expenses to credit cards would *cost* me money instead of *gaining* me money.

To execute this strategy, it is necessary to budget successfully to be sure that I have the income to cover all my credit card purchases, so that I am not charged interest and my credit score is not harmed.

Budgeting is important *all the time* because it determines your ability to save money which can be invested in stocks, a business, education, insurance against catastrophe, etc.. Your ability to budget determines whether you will lose money to interest fees and late fees, whether you will be able to save money by planning your purchases ahead and buying in bulk, whether you will build an excellent credit score or harm your credit score, etc.

All of these choices build up to determine your financial freedom. Do you have enough in savings to cover an emergency, make a down payment on a house, or pay for a high-quality education program that can change your career path in a way that brings wealth? Do you have enough money you aren't spending to invest in stocks that will grow with the market, making you more money while you sleep?

Budgeting is the cornerstone of all financial strategies because budgeting determines your ability to build credit, obtain good interest rates, save money to invest in your future wealth, etc.

This means budgeting is an important and excellent thing to learn if you haven't already, and creating tools that help people learn and execute budgeting is a fertile business opportunity. If you search Google for "budgeting apps" you will find countless businesses which make money by helping people budget without having to think too hard about it.

Budgeting is the most basic tool in the financial strategy toolbox, but as I mentioned here, to actually *gain* money instead of merely avoiding *losing* money, budgeting must be combined with knowledge of other tools. These include…

#2 Credit Scores

Your credit score determines what kinds of credit cards, loans, and other credit lines you have access to. Banks will use your credit score to decide how good of a deal to give you on homes, cars, and business loans, and entities like landlords and sometimes even employers use credit scores to decide how reliable and responsible of a person you are.

The tremendous advantages of getting good deals on home and business loans *alone* make cultivating a good credit score essential for financial success. A person with a poor credit score may be denied access to capital, housing, and even job opportunities, while a person with an excellent credit score and excellent financial strategy can profit tremendously by borrowing money.

Many commentators have pointed out that credit scores almost seem designed to perpetuate inequality: those with poor credit scores are often those who grew up in poverty, receiving no financial education while being forced to pay more money than they had to stay alive. Those who have excellent credit scores from an early age, on the other hand, are often the children of rich families who grew up with generational wealth and parents who taught them financial strategy.

Fortunately, it is possible to turn a poor credit score into an excellent one in just a couple of years: all that is needed is the necessary knowledge to create a credit-building strategy. Because of this, education about credit scores is an *excellent* thing to obtain if you haven't already.

It is also a highly lucrative business opportunity, with thousands of financial professionals around the United States running lucrative businesses built around educating people about credit and helping people to build excellent credit scores. When done properly, their clients end up richer than they started out, which helps these businesses to grow by creating new offerings and receiving new customers through their enthusiastic referral networks of previous customers.

We will discuss how credit scores are determined, and how they can be improved and used for profit, in more detail in the next chapter.

#3 Loan Terms

Much of our discussion so far has referenced home loans and mortgages, business loans, and credit cards as the key economic tools which move the economy. These are the tools which allow people who were *not* born wealthy to access tens or hundreds of thousands of dollars of financing that they can use to build wealth for generations of their family to come.

However, these are *also* the tools that banks worldwide use to make trillions in profit off of ordinary people, which is funneled into the hedge funds and investment portfolios of the already-rich.

How can both of these things be true?

The answer all comes down to "strategy." The rich profit hugely off of giving out loans because they calculate their loan terms such that people *usually* end up paying "back" far more money than they borrowed. Remember our home loan example from the previous chapter; under current interest rates, someone who purchases a $400,000 home would end up paying their lenders "back" more than twice what they borrowed to pay for their home.

For those who end up with a rapidly appreciating asset at the end of the process, this is still a good way to build generational wealth. With property rates rising as they have for the last several decades, that house that was purchased for $400,000 could easily be worth $800,000 or $900,000 in resale or rental value by the time its mortgage has been paid off.

But you still see the importance of strategy. We've already seen how a person with an excellent credit score can end up paying $100,000 less in interest for the same home. The same is true of business loans, credit cards, etc. Hundreds of thousands of dollars can be gained or lost several times over the course of a lifetime *by performing the same actions* depending on the terms a person receives on home loans, business loans, etc.

This is what it means to play the finance game. It means recognizing that $100,000 or more may be gained or lost in a 1% difference in the interest rates on a loan. It means strategizing to get the best interest rate on that loan through budgeting and credit building. Knowledge and strategy, or lack thereof, in these decisions is a major decider of which families become wealthy and which *lose* economic status.

For this reason, educating yourself about the terms offered by loans, credit cards, and other types of credit lines is one of the most powerful things you can do.

Fintech can help ordinary people to make the best choices by providing education, and even creating tools which automatically help people search and compare the loan options that are available for them. Countless businesses already exist in this space.

Consumer beware: some of these businesses have already been caught in shady deals where they were promoting less-than-ideal loan and credit card offers to consumers in exchange for kickbacks from lenders who wanted those sweet, sweet interest payments. For this reason, it is important to cultivate your own knowledge on these topics and not just assume that matching services must be giving you the best deal.

This might all seem a bit overwhelming right now, but keep this in mind: I'll bet the rules of your favorite game are also overwhelming to first-time players. Once a person has learned the rules and learned to benefit from them, learning more about the rules and figuring out how to use them to execute increasingly excellent plays becomes a *joy*.

Don't be put off of the game of finance by the initial difficulty in learning the rules. The rewards of becoming an excellent player are too good to pass up.

There are two more major tools in the wealth-building strategy toolbox whose importance to you, and whose potential as a business opportunity in the fintech space, I want to discuss briefly.

#4 Investing Skills

One secret of the wealthy is that they often invest their money in the stock market rather than leaving it in bank accounts. In fact, this is how most employer-provided retirement plans, such as 401ks and IRAs, work. In order to offer employees more money upon retirement, employers have qualified investment advisors invest employees' retirement savings into stocks which can double or triple in value before they are sold to pay for a person's retirement.

Unfortunately, investing can be a dangerous game, with many media outlets giving unreliable investment advice which may be colored by conflicts of interest. In the world of cryptocurrency, for example, those who already own cryptocurrency become wealthier when you invest in their cryptocurrency and raise its value. For this reason, many individuals and media outlets will encourage people to invest in cryptocurrency for strictly self-serving reasons.

For this reason, it is a good idea to work with a certified investment advisor, or at least do a great deal of research yourself, before deciding what stocks to invest your money in. Stocks can either gain or lose value, which means you can either gain or lose money as a result of investing in them.

At this time, Novae and I actually don't offer advice on how to invest in the stock market — that is not an area we've chosen to focus on. I have outsourced my own investments to a qualified investment advisor so that I know my money is well taken-care of without having to spend my own time watching the markets, and I suggest you do the same.

Still, I do want to mention investment as a wealth-building skill, because it is something that wealthy people overwhelmingly engage in, as it allows their money to grow instead of staying the same in a savings account. So if you find yourself with a lot of money in the bank, it may be worth putting that money into investment portfolios that are likely to grow with the market instead of letting it sit in a savings account.

There are also other types of investing outside of the stock market. Technology has made it easier to invest into real estate, and even into small businesses due to new concepts like crowdfunding. There are several ways to grow your money, from the convenience of your cell phone at home.

Please be cautious because this could be a complete blessing, or a complete curse. New methods of investment are often unpredictable, and may yield high returns one month but large losses the next.

It's important to remember that investing is capital- and knowledge-intensive, so before you start risking your hard-earned money in investment opportunities, it's important to build your knowledge and lean on the knowledge of investment professionals and mentors that you trust.

Finally, always remember, it's better to pay off debts that are charging you 25% in interest rather than attempting to find investments that could yield you 8% in returns. Where I'm from, they call that hustling backwards.

#5 *Business Skills*

Another major way to build generational wealth is perhaps the most powerful and most challenging of them all. This is the path of becoming a successful business owner.

Starting your own business has unlimited potential. The right idea for a highly scalable product or service that offers extraordinary value to customers, combined with the skills to execute that idea well, can easily make you a millionaire.

The "skills" part is where the challenge lies: to execute successfully, you must know how to:

1. Obtain startup capital

2. Provide and scale a high-quality product or service consistently

3. Successfully market your product or service in a way that generates many sales cost-effectively

4. Price and deliver that product or service in a way that is consistently profitable

5. Handle all of the necessary legal and financial paperwork to ensure that your product or service has the proper licenses for your city and state, meets all regulatory requirements, pays the proper taxes, etc.

If you are missing any of those pieces, your business is more than likely to fail. This is why *most* new businesses fail.

A major obstacle for new business owners is the fact that, as a first-time business owner, you often have hands-on experience with only one or two of the five essential skills listed above. Attending business school will give you academic knowledge of these requirements, but will not necessarily teach you how to effectively implement them in the real world. Working for a business you don't own may teach you one or two of these skills, but is unlikely to teach you all of them.

In other words, a *lot* is learned on the job. Many business owners learn from the failure of their first business, then go on to start a more successful one after learning those lessons.

I was fortunate to discover the direct sales industry as a young man, for one reason: the direct sales business model gives you experience with *almost all of those skills*. In many situations, sales professionals and direct sales affiliates are basically responsible for running their own businesses. They must find buyers, sell to them successfully, be thoroughly aware of the quality, features, and delivery timelines of the products they choose to sell, and be aware of the considerations that go into pricing these products for customers and businesses.

By entering the direct sales industry, I got a crash course in business skills from mentors who were more experienced in the field. This hands-on education helped me at least as much as my MBA when designing, starting, and growing Novae to be the four-times-running Inc 5000 business it has become today. And I want to pay that forward.

This is why I have started Novae University, which offers a crash course in sales and business skills with experienced mentors who are actively winning in the industry much more affordably than any business school.

Novae also offers an affiliate program, where we recruit ambitious individuals to sell Novae products and services, directly for us or as part of their own business models. In this program we provide on-the-job training in business skills, since your success is our success.

These programs are designed to be two of the easiest ways to get real world training in business skills while also becoming familiar with the fintech industry. No educational program guarantees that you won't make mistakes as a new business owner: all new business owners *do* make mistakes. But having mentors who are invested in your success can drastically cut down on these mistakes, and make it much easier for people who come at the endeavor of starting a business with rigor and an attitude of radical responsibility to succeed.

We won't have room to teach you about all of the bullet points we have listed in this chapter for how to gain wealth for yourself and your family through home ownership, investing, starting a business, and more. But you can see the opportunity here. There is enough to learn, and the knowledge is powerful enough, that there is a need for services that teach these rules, strategies, and skills to people who weren't taught them growing up.

With advancing technology, there are more and more ways to give people access to curricula using online learning, interactive lessons, and mentorship. And there are enough strategies to obtain wealth that there is room in the market for many different specialized curricula built around specific strategies for gaining wealth. As of this writing, the financial education space is still a relatively untapped market with tremendous room for growth.

Of course, not all online gurus or classes about money are to be trusted. Unfortunately because of the high demand for this information, there are people and organizations who have been known to lead their students astray. If you're seeking financial education for yourself, ask:

1. What do reviews on third party websites say about this company? Don't look mainly at the testimonials the company has selected to represent themselves. Instead, look on websites like Google Reviews, the Better Business Bureau, and other services not affiliated with the company to see what past students or customers are saying about them.

2. How much individual support does this program offer for students? Especially if the program teaches a highly challenging topic like starting your own business or starting work in a new industry, is there individual mentorship available, or direct access to business opportunities through the program?

3. Do you personally know anyone who has gotten results from this company? Sometimes you're the first in your

social circle to seek business or finance education, but students of excellent programs *that work* will often be eager to refer you to what worked for them.

I hope this chapter leaves you with a clearer understanding of how the wealthy *become* wealthy, and how you might pursue wealth yourself.

Which path sounds best to you? Do you want to become a homeowner or other real estate owner whose wealth will appreciate with rising property prices? Do you want to become a business owner whose business can be scaled to make almost unlimited amounts of money?

We will say more about the essential cornerstones of these processes, such as building your credit score and learning business skills, in the chapters to come.

Chapter 5

How Fintech Can Help You Build Credit

As we've seen in Chapters 1-4, having a good credit score is a prerequisite for gaining wealth. It is the first thing many financial educators talk about. In my case, I wanted to wait until after I had established what is possible for you to accomplish with financial strategy.

It is possible for you to own a home that may double in value in the next 20 years. It is possible for you to start a business with virtually limitless revenue potential.

In order to do these things, one of your most powerful allies will be an excellent credit score that gets you access to low-interest loans, credit lines, and rewards. And you can build yourself an excellent credit score, even if you have a very poor credit score right now.

In general, credit scores range from 300-850. They are designed to try to predict how likely a person is to pay back money lent to them in a timely fashion. This is important for lenders like banks and credit card companies to know because it determines their likelihood of making sweet, sweet interest on the money they lend you.

If you have a near-certain chance of paying them back, they know they will make lots of money off you in interest payments. As a result, they will try to lend you a *lot* of money, and they will offer you the lowest interest rate they can so that you will borrow it from them and not from somebody else. This is what happens when you have an excellent credit score.

If you have a low chance of paying them back, on the other hand, they will only lend you small amounts of money, and those at very high interest rates. They may still want a chance to collect interest payments from you, but they know that in order to do so they will have to charge you a lot of interest *fast*, because there's a chance that you won't make all your payments on the loan or credit lines. This is what happens when you have a poor credit score.

So how do you improve your credit score? Well, one thing to know (which strikes me as a bit frustrating) is that credit bureaus who create your credit scores are actually privately owned, for-profit businesses. They make their money off of selling information about how likely a person or business is to pay back loans to banks and other moneylenders.

This means that they keep their algorithms for determining credit scores secret. Each bureau's credit score calculating algorithm is basically their secret sauce. This means that if you ask, you will often be told that no one can tell you exactly why your credit score rose or dropped by a certain amount, because that would mean revealing how their super-secret algorithm works.

However, according to independent analysts who have studied credit score algorithms extensively from the outside, we can guess that the basic formula used by all three major credit bureaus that calculate personal credit scores (Equifax, Experian, and Transunion) goes something like:

- 35% payment history. This is the single most important factor in your credit score. If you pay all your bills on time, you will get full credit for this 35% of your score. If you often pay bills more than a month late, this score will suffer.

- 30% percent credit utilization. This score looks at how much of your available credit lines, such as credit cards, you are already using. If you keep your credit card usage under 7% (carrying a credit card balance less than 7% of your total credit limit on that card), you will get full marks on this section. If you use 20%, 30%, or even more of your available credit limit, this part of your score will suffer.

    This is especially true if you carry a 30%+ balance on any of your credit cards for more than a few months. This tells the credit bureaus that you may be struggling to pay your bills already, which will make new moneylenders less likely to want to lend money to you.

- 15% length of credit history. This simply means how long you have a track record of paying back money. The longer your credit history, the better this score will be. The logic behind this may be obvious: the longer you get to watch someone do something, the better an idea you have of how good they are at it.

  In this case, the more years you have spent successfully borrowing money and paying it back successfully, the more reliable a borrower you are considered.

- 10% credit mix. This looks at how many different *ways* you have borrowed money. Do you only have credit cards, or do you also have a home, business, car, or student loan, or a retail installment payment plan? While this may seem a strange thing to take into account, this tells creditors how good you are at paying off loans that have different kinds of terms.

  However, don't go out and get a loan just to raise this score! This is only a small part of your credit score.

- 10% new credit. This refers to how many new credit cards or other credit lines you have taken out recently. Opening multiple new credit accounts might indicate that you are having trouble paying your bills, which again could make you less likely to pay off future loans or credit cards successfully.

For this reason, you will want to be strategic when applying for financing for anything. We will talk more about how to do that in this chapter.[1]

Now you've seen that credit scores can actually be a bit complicated. Keeping track of all the factors that affect them, and how to have an optimal one so you can get the best financing for your home or business, is not always simple.

This is why fintech can help in this area. It can deliver education about how to improve your credit score, and help people track their credit score in real time with credit monitoring apps. Groundbreaking technology is even creating AI-powered software to automatically complete certain tasks that might help improve your credit score *for* you. We'll talk more about that later in this chapter as well.

For now, because we have started you on this topic, I would like to give you a brief primer on how to improve your credit score yourself. I will highlight ways in which fintech can help you overcome certain obstacles to doing so, but consider this your free crash course in the basic steps that *will* get you an excellent credit

---

1. *How are FICO scores calculated?*. myFICO. (2024, August 19).

score and open your door to excellent home and business loans if you accomplish them all consistently.

Step 1: Check Your Credit Report

The first step to knowing how to improve your credit score is knowing what it already is. Fortunately, the U.S. government requires all three credit bureaus to give us a full credit report annually through AnnualCreditReport.com.

You can get all three bureaus' free credit scores at once, or you can space them out and order a free report from a different credit bureau each month. This will allow you to track your progress over time without ever having to pay for credit monitoring. Since all three bureaus' credit calculating algorithms are believed to be very similar, the results of each bureau's report should give you a decent idea of what's on the others.

Your credit report will include your score, but will also include much more detailed information. It will show if you have any late or missed payments on your credit report, how much the credit bureaus think you owe in loans, and much more. These reports will give you an idea of what specific actions you may need to take to improve your credit score.

For example, it is sometimes possible to call a creditor who has put a negative mark for nonpayment on your credit report, and offer to pay them some or all of your owed balance in exchange for them asking the credit bureau to change the mark on your credit score to "paid as agreed." Many creditors are willing to remove derogatory marks in this way if it means they will get paid.

While you are looking at your report, you may notice some inaccuracies. These can be as minor as having the wrong middle name listed on your account to as major as having incorrect past addresses or even incorrect past charges on your account. People with common first and last names may even end up with the wrong person's credit information on their account! We will talk about how to write to credit bureaus and ask them to remove these errors in a few pages.

For now, make note of what parts of your credit report are great and what parts need work. You can work on them both by adding new credit history, and by bargaining with creditors and credit bureaus to remove existing derogatory marks.

Step 2: Pay All Your Bills On Time (Don't Worry, I Have Some Tips)

I know, I know. "Pay all your bills on time" may be easier said than done if you're in a tough spot financially. But I have some tips that can help you build positive payment on your credit report, budget to pay off your bills faster, and potentially lower your total debt payoff amount. These tips include:

1. First, make sure you are paying all your bills on time. If remembering to pay them regularly is a challenge, consider setting a calendar or phone alarm reminder to do so. Many companies now also offer autopay options that automatically deduct the amount of their bill from your

bank account on the due date.

Some companies may even offer slight discounts for using autopay. A budgeting app may also help if ensuring that you have enough money left in the bank when the time to pay your bills is a challenge. It won't always be comfortable, but it will give you tremendous financial power in the long run.

2. Next, make sure that all the bills you are already paying on time are counted toward your credit score. With services like Experian Boost and Rental Reporting, you can add your rent payments and other payments such as utility payments to your credit report as positive payment history.

Obviously, you only want to do this if you are able to pay these bills in full and on time reliably; asking for bills to be counted and then not paying them may make things worse. But for any bills you are paying reliably, you deserve to get credit for that work on your credit report!

3. If you have really distressed debt, consider seeking debt relief services. In this business model, companies with lawyers and legal and financial expertise negotiate on your behalf to get a lower payoff amount from your creditor. When a debt is distressed enough that a creditor believes

they may not get paid at all, they are often willing to settle for a lower payoff amount rather than get paid nothing.

In this way, debt relief companies can help you decrease the total amount of your debts if paying off the full amounts seems unrealistic.

4. Pay down your highest-interest debts fastest. In previous chapters, we've seen the enormous power that just a 1% or 2% difference in interest rates can have. To pay your debts off ASAP, then, prioritize paying down your debts with the highest interest rates as fast as you can.

Any loans, credit cards, or past-due bills you have should have a section that shows your minimum allowed payment, and one that shows what you will accrue in interest and late fees if it goes unpaid. Try paying as much as possible toward the highest-paying debts until they disappear, putting other debts on the minimum allowed monthly payment in the process if you have to.

Once your highest-interest debt has disappeared, move the money you *were* paying toward that debt to pay down the next highest-interest debt. And so on. You will be surprised by how fast your debts disappear if you are able to budget this way reliably. You may be more motivated to save and earn money if you can see that high-interest debt rapidly disappearing!

Think of this as a sort of gamification of paying your debts, where you create visible progress for yourself.

5. Look for tools that might allow you to build credit history by allowing you to open small credit lines without any credit check. These may include tiny low-limit "credit cards" that exist only so you can charge a few dollars each month and then pay the balance in full, or "loan" services that allow you to lend small amounts of money to *yourself* and then pay yourself back over time to build a positive loan payment history.

Novae has built relationships with reputable companies that provide these services. You can check out our website NovaeMoney.com at the time that you read this book to view our list of recommended credit-boosting services.

Step 3: Maintain Low Credit Utilization

As we mentioned briefly above, credit utilization is the amount of total credit you have available to you. This is an important quantity to get aware of, because low-limit credit lines like those being pushed by many businesses these days can adversely affect your credit score if you don't understand credit utilization.

Credit utilization is intended to show how much credit you have available to you to use in the event of an emergency. Low credit utilization shows a money lender that you have sufficient cash flow to cover your financial needs, and that you have a lot of credit available to draw on in case something goes wrong. Both of those make you someone that a money lender would very much like to lend money to, because it suggests that you will be able to pay them back in full, with interest.

It might be obvious why someone having a balance of $3,000 or $4,000 on a credit card with a $10,000 limit would be concerning. It suggests that they aren't currently making enough money to cover their expenses, and they don't have that much wiggle room in additional available credit in case something goes wrong. That means they're less likely to pay back money you lend successfully than someone with $700 or less charged to their $10,000 credit card.

However, the situation can get trickier with the increasing prevalence of credit lines that have limits of just $200 or $300, like those that are often offered these days by companies like Amazon, Venmo, and PayPal. Because the credit limit is so low, even a relatively small purchase using one of these credit lines can show up to the credit score algorithm as "high credit utilization". It only takes a $100 purchase to show up as 50% utilization on a $200 credit line, after all.

Let's take a brief look at how much you can charge on credit lines with various credit limits without surpassing the ideal 7% utilization rate:

- 7% of a credit line with a $200 limit is just $14. That's the maximum you can charge on that credit line without having higher-than-recommended utilization.

- 7% of a credit line with a $1,000 limit is $70. That's the maximum balance you will want to have on a credit card with a $1,000 limit if you want to optimize your credit score.

- 7% of a credit line with a $5,000 limit is $350.

- 7% of a credit line with a $10,000 limit is $700.

The better your credit score gets, the higher-limit credit lines you will be offered. While you may only be offered credit cards with $500 or $1,000 limits if your credit is not great right now, with excellent credit you may be offered credit cards with $10,000 or $12,500 limits routinely. This is because your excellent history of paying your debts gives money lenders faith that you can repay large amounts of money.

Because of the credit utilization factor, I do *not* recommend that people accept lines of credit with limits lower than $1,000, even if they are aggressively advertised to you. Small credit lines offered by retailers and money apps can easily result in "high utilization" derogatory marks even if you only spend $100. It just isn't worth the risk to your credit score to have access to a few hundred extra dollars of credit.

If you already have a high credit utilization rate, treat this as you would treat any other debt. Research to find out what interest rate you are paying on each of your credit card balances, and add each of them to the list of debts you are paying off, putting as much money as you can toward the highest-interest debt each month.

Once your credit score has improved significantly, you can contact your bank to ask for an increase to your credit limit. Many banks will happily grant one if your credit score has changed to show that you are now in a better position to borrow money. In this way, the same credit lines can become higher-limit credit lines, which in turn makes it easier for you to avoid high utilization since your total credit limit is now increased.

While you are working on making your credit utilization rate excellent, you can also...

Step 4: Dispute Items on Your Credit Report

Remember those mistakes you may have seen when you were checking your credit score earlier? You can contact credit bureaus and ask to have them removed.

In fact, it may sometimes be worth contacting your credit bureau and asking to have any negative mark on your credit score removed, *even if it's not a mistake*. This is because credit bureaus are legally required to address all requests for removal within a certain window of time. Sometimes, if they are struggling to address your request in a timely fashion, they may simply decide that removing the item you have complained about is the easiest way to respond to your request.

The sad truth is that mistakes on credit scores have become a huge problem. Research has shown the percentage of credit reports with blatant mistakes on them rising over the course of the last decade, until *more than half* of all people's credit reports contained at least one mistake in 2024.

Some of these mistakes are relatively harmless, but some can be devastating. You may have heard horror stories of people who have been denied homes, cars, business loans, and even jobs—only to find out upon investigation that they were being blackballed because a total stranger's unpaid debt had been mistakenly assigned to their credit report, or because they had a tiny unpaid debt they didn't even know about.

One woman was horrified to discover that she had been denied jobs for years and ultimately faced felony charges because her daughters forgot to return a VHS tape to an Oklahoma Blockbuster in the year 2000. The mistake should have been worth about $20, but through a series of technicalities involving state laws and the video store chain's late fee policies, it spiraled into something that the credit and legal systems viewed as a history of felony-level theft.[2]

While cases like this are mercifully rare, my point is this: check your credit report. You can't be sure that a mistake or other situation that could be corrected *isn't* adversely affecting your life if you don't know what's on your report. And if you find items that might be adversely affecting your credit score or your reputation, it's worth taking the time and effort to ask to have them removed.

This is one frontier where I expect to see a big growth in fintech opportunities in the coming years.

Last year, I was proud to make Novae one of the first companies to roll out an AI-powered software which identifies potential errors and derogatory items on your credit report, suggests dispute reasoning that has worked for past clients, and generates the appropriate dispute letters. The user can then easily print and mail these letters to the credit bureaus, which still unfortunately insist on using snail mail for important correspondence.

This technology is important because the procedures for choosing the correct dispute requests to credit bureaus can be burdensome and sometimes complicated. If a credit bureau replies by refusing to remove an item from your report, it might be necessary to submit more letters to them within a certain time window. These letters might also need to contain certain legal jargon citing the laws which require these items to be removed from your credit reports.

Because the process can be time-consuming and exasperating and require research, many people simply don't dispute errors on their credit report, or give up after receiving the first letter from the credit bureau declining their request. For millions of people, it's simply too much work to add to their to-do list.

AI-powered software has the power to improve this situation by handling the work of writing the disputes, keeping the consumer notified of changes, and providing a roadmap for how to handle the process of improving their own credit. This software can be built with knowledge of the legal statutes that must be cited to get the best potential results, and can automatically generate replies that you can print out and send, escalating your requests if a credit bureau refuses the initial request to remove a mistake or derogatory mark.

Because the labor is all done by AI, fintech companies can make this software available to ordinary people at a relatively low price while still turning a profit on it. The customers then benefit from a potential fast-tracking of their credit score improvement that would not have been possible without the software.

Software like this can't help much if customers are chronically failing to pay bills or keep their credit utilization low. But for people who are suffering from cases of mistaken identity, or who are working toward paying down their debts and building their positive payment history, software like this can help to clear mistakes and ancient history off of credit reports and clean them up.

You can of course learn more about Novae's AI software, called myNovaeDisputes Manager, which is the only one I currently vouch for, at NovaeMoney.com.

Step 5: Be Mindful of Your New Credit Applications

It's important to know that applications for new credit lines can look bad on your credit report. Obviously, everyone must make such an application every now and then. But each time you do it, it lowers your credit score a little bit for a while.

This is part of the credit bureau's algorithm because *lots* of applications for new credit can signal that someone can't currently pay their bills, meaning they may not be able to pay back any money that is leant to them.

One solution to this is obvious: don't apply for new credit cards or loans very often. However, one thing that can be insidious is that some actions you take as a consumer may register as "applying for a new credit line" without you even realizing it. For example, did you know that all the following can count as "applying for a new credit line?"

- Applying for certain Buy Now, Pay Later plans. Some companies structure their BNPL plans like a loan, and will send a hard query to the credit bureaus just as if you had applied for a new credit card.

- Applying for financing for a car or certain other big-ticket items. This can cause a *lot* of trouble because people who are comparison shopping may apply for financing at six different car dealerships in order to compare the financing offers they get, not realizing that each dealership will register on their credit report as a separate attempt to "open a new credit line."

- Responding to "pre-approved" credit card offers. Even if the credit card company was the one who sent *you* the offer, or if a credit-monitoring platform promises that you're already approved for the credit line, you accepting the credit line will usually register with credit bureaus as you "applying for a new credit line" and raise suspicion that you can't pay your bills.

As lending money becomes more and more popular as a business model, more and more different types of companies have begun inquiring about potential customers' credit and making it look like the customer is trying to borrow money over and over, even if that's not the customer's intent. Here are some tips you can use to prevent unwanted credit inquiries on your credit report:

- Before applying for any kind of auto financing or Buy Now, Pay Later, ask if the process will involve a hard inquiry on your credit report. If the answer is "yes," try to keep this kind of activity to only once or twice per year, if possible. More than three inquiries on your credit report within a six month period will almost guarantee a decline on most new applications for credit, even if the other areas of your credit are good.

  Most websites are required to disclose if their process will result in an inquiry on your credit, but they might hide it in the fine print of the terms of service or only tell you after you've completed most of the application.

- If you know you are buying a big-ticket item which may require a loan, apply through a fintech platform instead of asking individual sellers about their financing.

Doing this allows for a single soft pull on your credit to run your application through several banks, showing you which one may approve you without having to rack up several hard inquiries on your credit report. If you accept one of the loan offers, that will be when the hard inquiry takes place.

In this way you can already have financing in hand when you visit retailers, and you will only need one inquiry from the bank instead of the several you might accrue if multiple sellers inquire about your credit in order to make an offer. And if you find that you don't qualify for any low-interest offers at this time, then you can also find *that* out without sustaining several hard inquiries that might damage your credit further.

- Be strategic about when you *do* apply for credit or financing. Try to keep your new applications down to just once or twice a year, and really make them count. For example, you may wish to reserve your credit applications for high-limit credit cards with excellent interest rates and rewards, or for financing a major item that will last you many years like a new car.

In some ways, advancing technology is making the landscape more treacherous for consumers. Hard inquiries on your credit and high interest rates can now be hidden in places that didn't used to have those, and low-limit credit lines offered by apps and stores can harm your credit utilization score.

This is one reason why it is increasingly necessary to be vigilant about caring for your financial future, and one reason why I foresee the financial education and credit education industries as rife with opportunities for fintech companies to step in and make consumer's lives a little bit easier.

Step 6: Maintain a Mix of Credit Lines (If You Can)

Having a mix of different kinds of credit lines, such as credit cards and installment loans, can positively impact your score. Many of us manage this simply by having student loans, auto loans, home loans, or another type of loan that is paid over time in addition to one or more credit cards.

However, it is usually not worth taking out a large loan just to diversify your credit report. Credit mix is a relatively small part of your credit score, and taking out thousands of dollars in debt just to augment this piece of your credit score is likely to do more harm than good, especially if it is not managed correctly.

Instead, consider the following options:

- Keep older accounts open whenever you have the option to do so without taking penalties. Even if you have the option to close a credit card or completely pay off a loan ahead of schedule, consider keeping that card open and charging a monthly cup of coffee on it, or paying your loan down to a small amount and then stretching your final payments out as much as possible without being behind your payment schedule.

The key is to minimize the amount of interest you are paying as a result of the borrowed money and credit. It's all about the strategy. Paying off a loan can improve your debt-to-income ratio, which is important to qualify for larger loans later. But never, ever, close a credit card. You're not paying any interest and you're not penalized for having a $0 balance credit card open.

These ideas are especially helpful because credit *age* is also a significant factor in your credit score. If you close out an older credit card, this could actually hurt your credit score by effectively erasing several years of positive payment history from your report.

- If you have *no* credit cards, get one. Charge a cup of coffee, your gas, or your groceries on it and then pay it off in full each month. This will demonstrate that you have a positive payment history on a credit card without actually costing you extra money.

If you're very disciplined with your money, you can charge *all* your purposes to credit cards, and pay them off in full before the statement date ends to avoid interest.

By doing this with the right credit cards, you also can be rewarded—pun intended.

- See if you can become an authorized user on a family member's credit card or line of credit that is in good standing, if there is a credit line with a low utilization rate that can benefit your credit score instead of harming it. You wouldn't want to be added to a credit card or credit line that increases your debt-to-income ratio dramatically or increases your credit utilization.

If you are currently on someone's credit line that is making your credit score worse, consider getting removed immediately so your score won't continue to suffer. Note that this is a risky move to be a co-applicant or co-signer with someone to attempt to build your credit. By becoming a co-applicant or co-signer, you will *also* be legally responsible if the primary loan or card holder fails to pay their bills.

For this reason, it is generally recommended that you only co-sign an existing credit line for your own benefit, *not* because someone else asks you to because they don't have proven payment history themselves. Only undertake this with someone who you trust to have impeccable financial judgement, and while considering what impact the new loan or credit line has on your credit profile.

However, within financially savvy families, parents will sometimes make their newly adult children authorized users and or co-applicants on their credit cards or loans simply so that credit line can be added to the child's credit report as positive payment history. My wife and I actually practice this strategy in our family. My son, who is 23 at the time of the writing of this book, had a 785 credit score at the age of 18.

Step 7: Be Patient

Remember that building any kind of history takes time. This includes positive credit history. If credit scores could be boosted overnight, they wouldn't be a reliable measure of someone's financial dependability. Instead, expect it to take months to see major improvements to your credit score.

This doesn't mean you won't see your hard work pay off.

If you are following these instructions, you should have the satisfaction of seeing your debts and credit card balances shrink every time you are able to make a payment, seeing new positive payment history added when you add your rent and utilities payments to your credit reports, seeing letters sent off to credit bureaus asking them to remove derogatory marks, and potentially even seeing debt balances shrink and derogatory remarks removed as you negotiate with creditors.

But keep in mind that these factors can take time to affect your score. You may see small changes each month, or a big change occur suddenly after several months.

And all the while you will be building the habits that will lead you to long-term financial success. When you are firmly in control of your budget, your spending, and your payment habits, you can spend the rest of your life redirecting those skills to put your money into places that will empower you and your family for generations once your debts are paid off.

Step 8: Obtain a Credit Score of At Least 750

I personally recommend that people obtain a credit score of at least 750 before applying for bold financial moves such as buying a home or obtaining a business loan. This is because an excellent score of 750 or above will get you the lowest interest rates and the largest amount of money (depending on your income) when you do apply.

You don't want to take on a major, long-term debt when your credit score is lower than 750, because you will almost certainly end up paying much more back in interest in exchange for less value if you do. So be patient, and wait until the time is right to apply.

If you find it challenging to obtain this score prior to purchasing a home or securing funding for something you need sooner, go ahead and get the loan but continue working on your credit score to get it above 750. You can refinance your loan later to get the better rate.

Always shoot for the lowest interest rate possible so you can allocate your money somewhere else to build wealth, not pay expenses like interest.

Is Business Credit the Next Step for You?

Now that we have covered the basics of building personal credit, I want to tell you about something called business credit. Business credit is quite similar to personal credit: you can be given loans and credit cards for your business, and your business will receive its own credit score as a consequence. In many ways business credit is similar to personal credit for your business, but it has some important differences.

Business credit is one of the best-kept secrets of successful business owners. I have been privileged to teach about business credit at many conferences, as well as writing about it for Forbes.com. Business credit allows a strategic CEO to rapidly build their business's "financial capacity," that is, your business's total ability to obtain, spend, and make money.

We will go over the steps needed to obtain a business credit score and begin building your business's credit history as an independent entity from your personal credit soon. First, let's understand three things that make business credit vastly superior to personal credit when it comes to funding business ventures:

> 1. The limits are higher. Because it's natural for businesses to have higher expenses than a private individual, business

loans and credit cards often offer much more borrowing power than personal credit cards and loans. They may also offer unique rewards packages which can reduce some of your business's expenses to nearly $0.

2. Using business credit protects your personal credit score. Business credit is intended to stay with and represent the credit of your business, which, like all businesses, might undergo many changes of ownership and management over time. For this reason, your business's credit history will be counted as totally separate from your personal credit history.

This means that if something bad happens to your business, the financial hit will not affect your personal credit or assets. It is important to note that some business credit offers still check your personal credit profile, and show up on your personal credit report. This is called business credit with a "personal guarantee."

This is why it is important to maintain your personal credit score as a valuable asset for both personal and business use, even if you are also benefiting from a separate, excellent business credit score.

3. Most business credit cards' minimum payments are lower than the minimum payment percentage required by

personal credit cards. This means if cash flow is tight in your business at the moment, paying the debt back can be more manageable. Most business credit cards' minimum payment is around 1% of the total balance owed, while the average personal credit card minimum payment relative to the balance is around 2%-4%.

This could make or break a business in tough financial times. Your liability can vary slightly depending on how the business is set up—in sole proprietorships, for example, business owners may be held personally liable for business financial issues.

But for most types of business structures, you will be protected, and your business's credit history and borrowing power becomes part of the value that you can offer to buyers who may someday wish to pay you millions of dollars in exchange for ownership of your business.

Now, the reason I am telling you about business credit *after* telling you so much about personal credit is that banks are increasingly looking at the personal credit of a new business's founder when making decisions about lending to a business.

Even though you and your business will be two separate legal entities once you file the necessary paperwork, a new business with little to no credit history of its own may be asked to provide its owner's personal credit information in the same way that banks might ask a parent to co-sign the loan of a new adult with no credit history of their own.

For this reason, it is important that you work towards having excellent personal credit while starting to build business credit because you will need it if you'd like to move through the business credit building process faster. Once your business has built up its own credit history, your personal credit history will likely be seen as irrelevant. But when your business has no credit history of its own to stand on, your personal credit score will be important to determining the kind of funding your business can get. Most lenders will still want to know you are financially responsible in your personal life, making a soft pull on your personal credit to ensure the majority owner hasn't recently filed bankruptcy, have a legal judgement against them, and that you're not delinquent on federal or state taxes. If those things check out, your business will carry the liability of the financing.

Entire books can be written about how to incorporate your business as a legal entity of its own and build up its credit history to optimize the loan offers you are given. But for now, I do want to give you a brief outline of some steps you will need to perform. Our company specializes helping people to build business credit. Even if you don't work with a company like Novae, it's important to have a team of experts that can assist you or provide a fintech platform like ours to help accelerate the process. There are many steps for building business credit effectively, but for the sake of time, I will summarize them into four main categories. Here are the four categories that we share with aspiring entrepreneurs looking to build business credit with our help:

1. **Fundable Foundation.** To build business credit, you will need to start by incorporating your business as a legal entity. Which type of entity (LLC, S-Corp, etc.) is best for you will vary based on your business plan, so do some research about the pros and cons of each type of organization before selecting one.

   Once you have your EIN (Employer Identification Number, which is like a Social Security Number for a business—you get an EIN even if you have no employees), you can use this to open your first business bank account and take the first step to building your business its very own credit score.

   Here's a pro tip: when deciding what to name your business, check to see if the web domain "YourBusinessName.com" is already taken, and if there are already businesses with names similar enough to your own to potentially confuse customers.

   Many people get their heart set on a name or even file incorporation paperwork, only to realize that someone already owns their business's website domain or has a very similarly named business that confuses customers into working with the other business.

Our program for new and aspiring business owners breaks this "first step" down into 10 individual steps, but for this bite-sized summary, the overall goal is to establish a foundation for your business which will become eligible for funding through business credit.

2. **Business Credit Reports.** Once you have finalized your business's name, established it as an EIN, and performed other necessary steps, you will want to establish credit reports with the major Business Credit Reporting Agencies. These are the reports that will track your business's credit history, proving to lenders that your business is a great business to lend large amounts of money to.

This will include getting a D-U-N-S number, which is free, but you do need to make sure you file the proper paperwork to obtain one. A D-U-N-S number is necessary to establish your business credit report with Dun and Bradstreet, which is considered the gold standard of business credit bureau reporting by many lenders.

Experian Business and Equifax Business are other business credit bureaus you should get registered with as well. These bureaus also generate a business credit score that will be critical in your ability to obtain business funding.

3. **Initial Business Credit.** The first type of credit most businesses get is vendor credit, where vendors sell you supplies for your business on credit. This kind of credit is important for establishing the positive payment history you need to qualify for bigger, better lines of credit in the future.

Establishing positive payment history can be tricky, because 97% of vendors who sell to businesses don't report positive payment history to credit bureaus. For this reason, it's important to find at least a few vendors who *do* report to at least two of the three major business credit bureaus (which are Equifax, Experian, and Dun and Bradstreet).

We at Novae provide a portal with dozens of vendors that allow businesses to obtain business credit lines which can be used to not only fund the new business, but also build positive payment history, which builds your business credit score toward the point where you can get more and more flexible financing to grow.

Working with a company that provides you all the resources you need in one place makes the learning and growth curve much shorter for businesses, and is one of the reasons for Novae's continual success.

4. **Revolving Credit.** Once your vendor credit has established enough positive payment history to give you a good business credit score, it's time to think about revolving credit. This is a term for credit that allows you to borrow, repay what you borrowed, and then borrow from the same line of credit again.

   Think for example of credit cards where you can pay off the credit line and then charge more expenses to it, compared to a loan that you only receive once and cannot borrow again once you have repaid it.

   There are many types of revolving credit available to businesses, ranging from general use revolving credit lines like credit cards to product-specific credit lines such as fuel credit lines that can be used specifically to pay for gasoline for fleets of vehicles.

It's important to graduate through the additional 3 tiers of business credit, after the 1st one which was vendor credit. Department store credit, fleet credit, and lastly cash credit, complete the tiers. Once you have reached this stage, you have strong business credit that can allow you to obtain massive financing to grow your business. You are well on your way to building lasting generational wealth.

You can view a more extensive explanation of how to build your business credit by watching a 90-minute recorded webinar which is available for free on our website, NovaeMoney.com. Click on "Small Business," select the "Business Credit" page, and scroll all the way to the bottom to access this free 90-minute webinar.

If all this sounds intimidating, fintech platforms like Novae that specialize in business credit building provide user dashboards with easy access to these creditors. Fintech tools like this can monitor your business's credit growth and tell you exactly when to apply, based on your progress, to ensure approval and proper building of your business credit profile.

If you'd like to learn more about the tools Novae offers for new or growing business owners, you can visit NovaeMoney.com and click on Small Business.

Don't ever let a business tell you that you *have* to work with them in order to succeed. That just isn't true. But it can help a lot to have some expert support when you are getting started, since the knowledge gap is the number one reason why people who aren't raised rich don't usually *become* rich in their lifetimes.

Once your business has its own excellent credit history established, the very best in business loans and credit lines will be within your reach. An excellent business credit score means access to loans and credit lines with tens or hundreds of thousands of dollars, available to you with generous repayment terms and low interest rates.

Now we're really talking about building generational wealth.

Go Forth and Build Wealth!

I hope that this list can serve as a jumping-off point for further research for aspiring entrepreneurs and business owners.

I also hope that this chapter illustrates the power of financial education—and gives you an idea of why financial education, and tools that assist people in automatically performing some of the steps described in this chapter, are such promising business opportunities.

Imagine how much value can be conveyed, how much wealth can be built, and how much profit can be made from systematically teaching these facts and guiding people through the process of building personal and business credit! And the creative use of digital technologies such as AI has the potential to make such programs infinitely scalable.

Chapter 6

How Fintech Gives You Access to Opportunity

So much of opportunity in life is about money. Anyone who has been alive for very long has seen that. Whether the question is how safe your neighborhood is, what schools you can go to, what vacations you can take, or whether you can afford to retire, money determines what opportunities you have access to.

As much as the popular myth of American meritocracy claims wealthier people are just smarter and work harder, this simply isn't true. While a percentage of America's wealthy *are* self-made individuals who have educated themselves and worked their way to wealth, most people in America who are wealthy are wealthy *because they were born wealthy*, and subsequently had access to the best financial knowledge, schools, neighborhoods, etc. from early in life.

This may sound depressing, but it's a fact that we must address in order to understand how fintech changes the equation. Through the power of fintech to convey financial education and help people build business and personal credit as well as business-building skills, it becomes possible for just about anyone to build a scalable business that translates into wealth or opportunity.

With proper knowledge of the financial system, you no longer need to *have* tens or hundreds of thousands of dollars in order to own property or a business. You can learn how to *obtain* tens or hundreds of thousands of dollars, and turn that money into millions and tens of millions, by learning how to climb the credit ladder and turn money into profit.

We've covered how one goes about obtaining financing to invest in personal or business wealth, and how fintech can help, in some depth in the previous chapters. So now I want to address the piece that may still be missing in your understanding of how to turn loans and other forms of financing into profit. I want to address how you learn business skills.

"Business skills" refer to a wide range of skills you need to successfully turn loans into profit. Some examples of skills that are needed to accomplish this include:

- Budgeting skills, including the ability to factor required licensing fees, tax payment, and labor costs into your budget.

- Market analysis skills which enable you to see unmet

needs in the market and create products or services that meet those needs.

- Product design skills which enable you to figure out how to make a product highly profitable, such as by ensuring that the pricing yields a generous profit margin after covering all the costs of parts and labor to create the product.

- People skills, including knowing how and when to trust workers and experts, how to get along with and manage people, and how to build expectations in your employees and business partners that will lead to profit.

- Legal knowledge to ensure that you don't run afoul of the law, and may even be able to use it to your advantage.

- Big-picture thinking which allows you to plan and execute a successful scaling of your business, allowing it to grow and continue growing your family's generational wealth.

That's a lot! But don't worry: you can handle it. You just need the proper environment, mentorship, and incentives to ensure that you succeed on this steep learning curve.

What do I mean by "environment, mentorship, and incentives?" Let's break down each term, and how they can make or break your ability to master the challenging yet supremely rewarding skills of running a successful business.

Environment

The environment you find yourself in has a huge amount of influence over what you can and will do with your life. While it is possible to succeed in almost any environment despite long odds, a few things make you less likely to be wildly successful in business.

One of those things, ironically, is comfort. There's a reason we hear a fair number of "rags to riches" stories, but fewer "middle class to riches" stories. People who did not grow up learning the skills of successful business ownership *and* who are comfortable where they are right now rarely decide they must change their entire lives in order to become wealthy.

In fact, in this respect you can turn being in a desperate situation into an asset. If you are extremely motivated to accomplish financial security and turn that security into prosperity, you will get more done than someone who may have it easier in life—and who may choose not to become an Inc 5000 CEO precisely because they don't *have* to.

The same goes for your social circles. If you are surrounded at all times by people who are content with their current place in life and who prefer to relax and have fun in the same old ways rather than work hard at personal development, you are likely to be tempted to behave the same way they do.

People around you will shape your idea of what behavior and expectations are "reasonable," and if you believe that the intense work and study required to become a successful business owner quickly is "unreasonable," you probably won't do it.

And that might be fine for you! But keep in mind that who you spend time with matters. And being in a desperate situation doesn't *hurt* your chances of becoming a successful CEO. In fact, being desperate may *help* you become a successful CEO if you can harness that motivation to become excellent at turning financing into profit.

Mentorship

Having motivation and desire is essential to becoming a successful CEO. But you are probably still wondering, "What are these skills that I have to learn in order to be a successful CEO? Where would I even start learning them?"

This is where mentorship comes in. You can read all the books in the world, but knowing exactly how to put that knowledge into practice in real-world situations will remain hit-or-miss until you have actually started doing business—with someone who has already learned to excel in business at your back.

Once you begin taking the steps to create your own business, you will swiftly be confronted with exactly the questions that you need to ask, and find the best answers to, in order to succeed. And your chances of finding the right answers will be much greater if you can ask someone who has faced this exact question or situation before.

This is why I love the direct sales business model so much. In direct sales, you usually work under the mentorship of a more experienced sales professional who can tell you with real-world wisdom exactly what you, personally, need to do to up your game and succeed. Mentors can give you exercises and provide you with opportunities (or throw you into them, in some cases) that trigger massive growth.

Few industries or environments *other* than the direct sales industry accomplish this so intensely. Business school doesn't really offer the same boots-on-the-ground real world experience; most jobs don't have an interest in helping you grow as a business owner, but only as an employee who follows orders. In direct sales business models, however, very often more experienced business owners and professionals have direct incentive to help you succeed as quickly and effectively as possible.

Speaking of which, let's examine the ways in which the direct sales business model powerfully incentivizes you to learn and grow your real-world abilities.

Incentive

It is an interesting fact that people whose first career rewards them in direct proportion to the effort they put in are more likely to be wildly successful later in life. This is important because most jobs *don't* reward you in proportion to the effort you put in: generally, as long as you do enough to avoid getting fired, you get paid about the same in most job titles whether you give 50% or 110% at work.[1]

Unfortunately, as you may have experienced, even extreme com-

---

1. Gladwell, M. (2015b). *Outliers*. Manjul Publishing House.

petence and productivity often aren't rewarded *if you are an employee*. In fact, companies and managers might specifically *not* want to promote their best employees, because they are so good at the work they are doing in this specific role that they don't want to lose them in that role.[2]

However, extreme competence and productivity *are* rewarded if you own your own business, or if you work in direct sales.

Most sales professionals work on commission (they receive a percentage of the sales they make instead of or in addition to a constant salary) *because* businesses know that this kind of incentive model is the best way to promote success in workers. They break out this compensation model where it counts the most for the business's overall revenue, which is in the sales of products and services that yield very high commissions.

This is why I love direct sales as a training industry for new business owners. Not only does it give them more meaningful mentorship opportunities than almost any other job role, but it also teaches them through experience that hard work translates directly into wealth. It teaches the mindset that the harder you work and the more critically you think to optimize your processes, the more money you will make with less effort.

That's a great model! That is the core of optimization. The same thinking that will result in success for direct sales will translate

---

2. Harragan, B. L. (1992). *Games Mother Never Taught You*. Warner Books.

to success as a business owner in almost any industry you should choose to start a business in. Business ownership and direct sales both involve the same attitude of radical responsibility for your customers and your cash flow.

So where can you find opportunities for mentorship in direct sales, or other business models? Let's discuss how fintech can help with this as well.

Novae University and the Affiliate Program

I experienced the power of direct sales mentorship myself as a young man coming out of McDonough, Georgia. While I had always been ambitious and hard-working, I had not exactly been surrounded by examples of wildly successful wealth acquisition growing up. Most people I knew struggled to make ends meet, and those who had long-term vision saw college as the path to a better life.

They weren't wrong, exactly. My college and graduate degrees *did* help me make Novae what it is today. But imagine my surprise when I entered direct sales looking to make a little extra income and found myself surrounded by people who were making more money than my business school colleagues!

My colleagues and professors spoke about earnings and profit margins as academic figures written on pieces of paper; my direct sales colleagues casually chatted about their daily, weekly, or monthly earnings, and they were saying things I could hardly believe. When I asked them how they earned so much, often without a college degree, they'd tell me, keep it simple and follow the system.

I found that learning from people who were already successful in business and following the game plan they laid out was much more effective at producing results than my business school classes which covered complicated hypothetical scenarios. Once I began to have major success as a direct sales professional, I brought in other people, who in turn brought in more people, and taught them to be successful as well.

My work at Novae is strongly influenced by the concept of paying it forward. Just as I was granted mentorship and opportunities in the direct sales world that allowed me to become who I am today, I strive to make sure that the same opportunities are available to others systemically through programs like Novae University (we'll get to that in a minute), mentorship calls, and our channel partnership programs like our Affiliate Program.

The fact is, few people will get an MBA. MBAs are very powerful tools to succeed in business, but they are also expensive, time-consuming, and at least as much of their curriculum is designed to help a person work as a high-level employee in a big company as to help a person start their own business from the ground up. That might be ideal for you if you are looking to have a high income without all the responsibility of business ownership, but it is also limiting.

Most people *do* endeavor to earn life-changing incomes. And getting an MBA, speaking as someone who has gotten one, isn't necessarily even the *best* way to do that, let alone the most accessible.

The experience earned going from a novice direct seller to multi-million dollar earner in the direct sales industry couldn't be replaced by what I learned in the classroom earning my MBA. The resilience needed to stay the course, the communication skills needed to persuade, motivate, and lead people, the stamina needed to travel from city to city and do conference call after conference call—all that couldn't be gained from the classroom.

Without the experience of success as a direct seller, my MBA wouldn't have gotten me the level of success I have today. Most of my former classmates, unfortunately, aren't CEOs of Inc 5000 companies. They have not had the same boots-on-the-ground experience of practical problem-solving and independent leadership and success.

And from a certain perspective, this is *great* news. It's great because it means that the most important component of my success as a business leader is something that's much more accessible and easier to administer than an MBA program. Even now, I probably don't have the funds to run a major graduate school; I do have the funds, skills, and people power to run an easily scalable direct sales company and provide the most important aspect of my own formation as a business owner for countless other people.

I want to make one thing very clear. There are *many* classes and "university" programs out there claiming to offer a boot camp in a business model, financial skill, or other high-paying skill set that will make you rich. Some seem to be legitimate; I've heard good things about many coding boot camps. Others are almost complete scams that will take thousands of dollars from you and leave you with few marketable skills.

Many of these experts are in videos on social media driving exotic cars, walking out of luxury homes or talking about their program from a yacht. Their goal is to impress you by flaunting the wealth they have achieved. But in reality, several of these influencers have been caught *renting* luxury cars, homes, and boats to create a false appearance of wealth. And anyone who is well-versed in finance knows that constantly renting flashy luxury cars is not the way to build generational wealth.

It's extremely important to understand, to succeed, it's not about what someone can show you. What they actually teach you, and how well those teachings work when you apply them, is far more important. Anyone can fake the appearance of wealth for the time that it takes to shoot an advertisement. It's more important that your coach or mentor has truly gained the success you're looking for.

Be wary of the flashy business coaches. Remember, Warren Buffet lives in a middle-class suburb in Omaha, Nebraska. He knows that status symbols don't correspond to real wealth or power, and are often used to mislead people.

Listen well to one thing: unless you inherit wealth or win the lottery, *there's no such thing as* "effortlessly rich." Everyone who is successful in any business model works their butt off to obtain that success. The more "effortless" a guru or teacher makes their wealth program sound, the more likely it is that they are misleading you in order to make some effortless money off of you.

With that out of the way, let me tell you about Novae's education and channel partnership programs. Turning these programs into success *does* require effort; but when effort is applied, they have a very high success rate! Keep in mind that I am sharing these programs here because I designed them myself based on my experience: I may be a little bit biased, but they are the programs I feel most comfortable vouching for since I literally built them from the ground up myself.

Novae University

The easiest way to connect with Novae's educational offerings without making a long-term commitment is through Novae University. While it's important to note that our "university" is not an academically accredited institution that will give you a college or graduate degree, it is a program that offers intensely practical learning experiences for aspiring business leaders.

Novae University puts on programs such as the Blueprint for Success Seminar, Champion Speakers Boot Camp, Communication Pro Workshop, Women that Win Conference, MENtality to Win Conference, Advanced Sales Mastery, and Legacy to Leadership Summit. These events give you the opportunity to be surrounded by like-minded people who know that they can achieve success and prosperity—and who know that you can too.

Our Communication Pro Workshop focuses not just on communication skills, but also on selling skills and the skills necessary to lead more productive, peaceful lives. People are most likely to be persuaded by those who are happier than them, after all, so helping our students lead happier lives actually benefits our selling process.

The workshop also focuses on helping individuals learn how to communicate with other people from their perspective, with the goal of improving communication to bridge gaps and create better relationships both personally and in business.

Our Champion Speakers Boot Camp is exactly what it sounds like: a boot camp which puts you through rigorous exercises and experiences to hone you into a great public speaker. Experiences like these are priceless because if shyness or adrenaline are part of your public speaking challenge, the *only* way to learn to push through those is through hands-on experience with some intensely friendly peer pressure to go for the gold at your back.

During this boot camp, attendees also team up and prepare and present a seminar. The groups compete against one another with their new found skills in a speaking competition where a winning seminar group and a Champion Speaker are crowned.

As of the last few years, Novae University is also proud to offer Women That Win and MENtality to Win retreats, where we offer safe spaces to discuss the unique challenges to success that men and women face due to the social dynamics of our society. My wife and I have faced our share of these challenges, and we lead discussions about how we have overcome harmful messaging from society to step into power and healing.

Once per year, a summer event is capped off with an All White Party on a megayacht, where we offer hundreds of attendees a taste of the good life that is available to you if you apply your mindset and accomplish success.

What many people underestimate about business—and the reason they don't become highly successful business owners—is the power of mindset. It's easy to talk about whether someone has money to invest or knows how to file legal paperwork. It's harder to talk quantitatively about how much someone believes in their ability to have success, how prepared they are to take radical responsibility for their outcomes, and how motivated they are to learn and then actually do new things.

This, in my experience, is what the direct sales industry has that graduate school lacks. It is not something that's easily scored on a test or attested to with a certificate, but a person's growth mindset and motivation is *the single biggest factor* in their success, in my professional opinion. Mindset determines, not what a person has accomplished or knows how to do, but what they *will* accomplish and what they *will* know a year or a decade from now.

Mindset is what creates massive success stories, and it is what the direct sales industry excels at cultivating. Novae University is designed to introduce you to that mindset.

If you allow yourself to be open to the idea that success is possible for you, these can be life-changing experiences for people at any point in their career path. You will find an attitude of success and achievement, and access to expertise, that you are unlikely to find in your average office or university classroom.

The most value, though, can be obtained from our three channel partnership programs: the Affiliate, Co-Brand, and White Label Programs. These programs allow you to actually begin doing business in the field of fintech direct sales—the single most promising business model of our time, in my experience, which is why my wife and I have chosen it for ourselves—with mentorship and technical support from us at Novae.

The Affiliate Program

Novae's Affiliate Program allows anyone, no matter your experience or background, to enroll on our website as an affiliate. We will set you up with a website under your own chosen username which allows you to sell Novae services on commission. All you really have to do is the work of direct sales: the more people you refer to utilize our services through you, and they get started, the more you get paid.

This sounds deceptively simple, but remember that it's the same business model I started my business career under. The process of finding new customers and making sales is anything but simple, and will allow you to build the most powerful skills needed to identify sales opportunities, find underserved people, and design and offer services that actually help those people if and when you choose to start your own business.

The Novae Affiliate Program takes the work of creating and branding an excellent product off your plate for the first step of your business journey in order to allow you to focus on the business skills that, in reality, matter most. The best, most beneficial product in the world will not sell itself: sales opportunities need to be identified and executed successfully, and those are the skills you will work on building through practical experience in the Novae Affiliate Program.

It's also important to note that there are people that earn consistent commissions from Novae by being professional referrers. They don't consider themselves selling anything; they simply continue referring people to our services like they'd refer people to a good restaurant or movie.

The Co-Brand Program

The next level of partnership we offer is our Co-Brand program. Because this program requires more business skill and independence on the part of the applicant to succeed, we won't enroll just anyone. You have to apply and be approved for this one.

This program is usually best for people who already have or have been developing their own brand in the business world. It allows such people to begin developing their own unique business model and brand while still offering Novae products to attract people to their business.

Once you have applied and been approved, you pay us a setup fee to build a website with your own brand front and center. This website is "powered by Novae," which means that they can market our products and services while maintaining their own brand identity and leveraging our credibility and expertise.

This can be an excellent way to grow an existing business with added value and mentorship. It's a great way to take your first steps toward creating your own brand in the financial space without all the research, overhead, and risk associated with the new venture. It can take less than two weeks to get set up. And now, a business that once had one or two offerings, can now have over a dozen with no added overhead but multiplied earning potential.

The White Label Program

The highest tier of partnership we offer in independence and business-building for entrepreneurs in the financial technology space is our White Label Program. This program is for businesses that want to focus on their own branding while still being able to offer Novae products and services, marketing to the public under their own brand, while Novae and its partners do all the work necessary to administer Novae products and services to their customers.

White Label partners are also able to offer their own unique products and services alongside Novae's. This allows them to build awareness for their unique products and brands while adding Novae services to the value they are able to offer customers. It's a great deal for everyone involved: the business owner gets to add value to their website and company, the customer gets added value, and Novae gets referrals.

This is the most expensive of the options we offer: to be frank, we spend a good bit of time with the new partner diving into how they want their brand to be positioned in the marketplace, build a custom website for this new venture and even provide direct contracts with our exclusive partnerships. It's a level of mentorship and support that is not available to most business owners.

White Label partners have the option to either partner directly with Novae's other partner service providers under their own contracts, or opt out and operate under Novae's service agreement. As with all things in business, with more independence comes more power but also more responsibility.

I'm pleased to report that many of the people in our White Label program today began as members of our other Affiliate program. The Affiliate program allowed them to hone their business skills and build their brand with the support of sales commissions from marketing Novae, and many are now well on their way to success as independent fintech business owners.

The progression of opportunities Novae's channel partnership programs offer are inspired by Robert Kiyosaki's Cashflow Quadrant teachings, supporting our partners in gaining the independence and the business mindset to be able to turn their ideas into passive income over time through the sales of products and services.

This is the style of thinking that allows people to build more wealth than they ever could by trading their labor for a fixed amount of hourly income, and it is easier than ever to adopt this model of thinking in this digital age where a growing number of products and services are automated.

The question in the digital age is now simply this: are you going to be an owner of some of those automated processes, profiting off of the value they create? Or not?

With Novae's partner programs, I have done everything in my power to make ownership of the digital means of production accessible to nearly anyone.

Mindset and the Question of Ownership

I've made it pretty clear throughout this book that I believe direct sales, specifically in the fintech industry, is the single best business model for anyone to get into. After all, I didn't inherit this business model, or fall into it by chance: I chose it because it had the best potential for earning, personal development, and community service all at the same time.

However, I do want to close this chapter with one last note of encouragement. Even if you do not feel called to work in fintech, I do believe that getting experience with seminars and channel partner programs like those I've described here will assist you in accomplishing *any* business endeavor you undertake in the future.

There's no substitute for the impact that experiencing success has on the nervous system. Our nervous system often decides what we *can* do, and what is worth even trying, based on its level of past success experiences.

When we experience actually making money and growing a business, our brain doesn't just learn the necessary skills to accomplish those goals: it believes that we are capable of accomplishing those things, and applies our efforts accordingly, for the rest of our lives.

For this reason, I strongly encourage those who are interested in undertaking *any* business model to consider at least undertaking an apprenticeship in fintech direct sales. It is probably the easiest and most profitable field to learn business skills in, and, even more importantly, to obtain your first formative experiences of success in business.

These are experiences you will carry with you for the rest of your life, and they will forever reshape your own self-image and confidence.

Chapter 7

How Fintech Can Help Solve The Debt Crisis

Now it's time to address the elephant in the room. The United States is currently in the midst of a debt crisis in every possible sector, and it's only getting worse. I hate to sound like a pessimist, but anyone who can do math can see it: something's got to change, because eventually, something's going to give.

The U.S. government currently owes $36 trillion to various parties. While that number is a little bit deceptive—remember what we've learned so far, that not *all* loans are bad for the borrower—it certainly does make it clear that Uncle Sam isn't exactly swimming in money to bail We The People out of the debts that we owe to megacorporations and billionaires.

Talking about *who* we owe money to is important. Those who say that money is really just an artificial construct, a set of numbers on a balance sheet, are to some extent correct. There is no finite quality called "money" that the world is someday going to run out of.

Instead, money is more like a promise. A paper bill or a number in a bank account represents a certain amount of value or labor that we have promised or been promised. Currency is simply a way of representing amounts of labor and value in an interchangeable way, so that you can trade a $100 bill for something instead of trading some very specific task or item that the person selling the item happens to want.

This explains a lot about our debt problem. Since money is just a symbol for a promise, it can sometimes cease to have meaning. What does it even mean to charge someone $3,000 for an ambulance ride or $500,000 to cure their cancer? What does it mean to charge someone $250,000 for a graduate school education or $1,000,000 for a house?

These are amounts of money so large that they become arbitrary. The question being asked is not the practical question of "how much did this thing cost to produce?" or the civic duty question of "what is the lowest price for which I can provide a high-quality product or service?" Increasingly, in our economy, the question being asked is, "How much can I possibly persuade people to promise to give me in the future in exchange for this good or service?"

This has become a really big problem in America. As of this writing in December of 2024, Americans have cumulatively promised to pay $220 billion in exchange for past medical care, $17.9 trillion in exchange for their housing, $1.6 trillion for their past education, and $1.17 trillion to their credit card companies.

And, as many commentators have pointed out, this isn't just bad for the people who have to pay these debts back.

Unregulated medical expenses discourage people from seeking medical care, even when they have potentially life-threatening symptoms. Sky-high housing expenses discourage Americans from even trying to own property and lead to high rates of homelessness. Charging a small fortune for higher education discourages education, which leads to less educated and less innovative workers, voters, inventors, and politicians in future generations.

Wealthy investors have taken to trading debts like a person's medical debt or home loans as profit-yielding assets among themselves. The more interest you have gotten a person to agree to pay, and the longer you've gotten them to agree to pay it *for*, the more passive income and wealth you will accrue as the sort of wealthy person who can afford to buy other people's medical debts and profit from them.

So the cost being charged for essentials like medical care, housing, and education no longer have anything to do with how much it costs to supply those products and services: now it's about how much the ultra-wealthy members of the owning elite can convince ordinary people to pay them for the rest of their lives. This is why many other countries are paying much, much less for these same commodities than Americans are today.

Our government has occasionally tried to make laws against these practices similar to the consumer protection laws which exist in the European Union, but these laws so far have barely made a dent. While I am obviously a very pro-business person, I can also do math. This means I recognize that the current system of totally unregulated pricing for the essentials of life is not sustainable, and will eventually destroy our society if we let it.

But what in the world can fintech do about it?

Well, remember how I said the prices of many of these commodities have more to do with how much companies can convince people to pay for them than how much they cost to produce? This means that when companies realize a person is not going to be able to pay a debt, things get very interesting. This is where fintech has the ability to intervene and drastically reduce the debt burdens of individuals in distress.

What Happens to Distressed Debt?

Debt that has gone unpaid for a while is called "distressed debt." The longer a person goes without paying a debt, the less likely it becomes that they ever will. Their original creditor then starts thinking about how they can make money off the debt, even if the person never pays it.

The solution is to sell the debt. By selling the debt to someone else, they can get *some* money where they might otherwise have gotten none. The company they sell the debt to will then attempt to collect on the original amount of the debt, often using aggressive tactics such as bombarding the debtor's home or business with phone calls and threatening to damage their credit score.

This is the model behind most debt collection. Debt collection companies profit by buying debts for pennies on the dollar, and succeeding in collecting the original amount of the debt in some percentage of cases.

The end result of this model is that most distressed debts don't get paid, people with distressed debt have a miserable time being harassed for their money, and debt collection companies manage to profit even though they're not the original service provider and the original service provider does not receive the money the debt collector collects.

There is a much kinder model that has been gaining popularity in fintech spaces in recent years. In this model, debt relief companies step into the shoes of debt collectors: they don't buy distressed debt for pennies on the dollar and then demand payment of the full original amount owed from the borrowers.

Instead, debt relief companies are hired *by the borrowers* to negotiate the debt amounts owed with the creditors and reduce the total debt, immediately reduce the monthly debt payments, and consolidate all debt payments into one that will serve as a deposit into one account paying toward the total debt payoff that was negotiated.

Imagine that instead of being sent to collections for an unpaid debt, you call up a debt relief company. They will then call up your creditors and negotiate with them, using their knowledge of the law and economics to get the creditor to agree to lower the total amount of money they are asking of you in return for a guaranteed payout.

These debt relief companies are effectively negotiating with the creditor for them to sell your distressed debt *to you* for a reduced amount, instead of selling it to a debt collector. The company then gets paid a percentage of the debt reduction they've negotiated for you. Their fees are folded into the payments you make on the reduced debt amount, so you pay nothing up-front.

This business model doesn't *erase* debts, but it does take a big chunk of the investor profit out of the amount that consumers are expected to pay. And it does it without harassing the payer or leaving original creditors unpaid.

Remember that the providers can afford to take these hits: since pricing these days often has more to do with "what is the maximum amount we can get people to agree to pay" than "how much does it actually cost to provide the service," many providers of goods and services can afford to offer drastically reduced payoff amounts, as long as they get paid *something* by each customer.

This debt relief business model is rapidly gaining popularity today, for obvious reasons. It's an opportunity for people with the right knowledge to make money by offering their knowledge and negotiating skills to people with distressed debt in return for a lower payoff amount. Fintech is helping by facilitating connections between debt relief agencies, law firms, and people with distressed debt who need some relief.

This is a service that Novae is now proud to offer. You can schedule a free consultation for our debt relief services at https://FreeDebtHelp.com. These are one of the services you can offer customers if you become a Novae partner. We even offer a special, free partner program for this service in particular. You can learn more about earning money by referring people to our debt help program at https://FreeDebtHelp.com/Partners.

We aren't the only ones offering these services. You may have seen ads for these services and assumed they were too good to be true. And I can't promise you they're not. There are predatory businesses in this field, just like there are in every other field, and I can't vet each and every one.

What I can tell you is that, when it comes to Novae's services, we have maintained our growth by maintaining an excellent reputation. We are big believers that long-term success for a business depends on actually delivering excellent customer experiences consistently, rather than the model some businesses espouse of extracting as much cash as they can from customers quickly and only worrying about the long-term when trouble starts as a result of a poor reputation. Since even debt relief programs can be predatory, here are a few red flags to watch out for when choosing a credible debt relief company that is likely to save you money rather than costing you more:

#1 Avoid Companies That Pressure You

One extremely popular sales tactic these days is time pressure. These are the ads that claim that you can only get a great offer for the next few hours. These ads may literally have a ticking countdown clock on the screen to make you feel a sense of urgency to buy the product right away.

In my opinion, this tactic is almost always a red flag. It is designed to pressure people into agreeing to something without allowing them to do research on the seller or carefully consider their option. By promising (usually falsely) that you can *only* get a good offer if you sign up *now*, companies can get customers to buy without researching their credentials or comparing their offers and reputations to those of other companies.

Reputable companies who genuinely have a great product to offer typically have no need of such tactics. In fact, because of their good word-of-mouth, you may hear about great companies from satisfied customers who are actually people you know, rather than from an online ad that pressures you buy *now*.

Anyone who wants to rush you into a decision probably doesn't have your best interest in mind. They want you to make a decision without having the chance to consider all of your options, or take time to learn about the potential consequences.

This holds true in life as well as in business.

#2 Avoid Companies with Up-Front Fees

In many states, it is actually illegal to charge up-front fees for debt relief services. However, this is not true in all states, and it doesn't stop some companies from trying.

Before agreeing to debt relief, or *any* other service arrangement, carefully read the contract and all informational materials to make sure you understand the fees and costs associated. Too many unscrupulous advertisers *imply* that something is free that you actually have to pay for, or state that the service is free for *some* people and then tell you you're not one of them.

Debt relief is one of the industries where *no* credible company should charge you an up-front fee. If they are actually good at what they do, they will be able to take their fees out of the reduced debt payoff amount they get for you. If they ask you for money up-front, this suggests that they aren't actually confident that they will be able to get you a reduced payoff amount so they want you to pay them just for making an effort which may be not achieve any results for you.

#3 Avoid Companies that Promise Fast and Easy Money

As with most industries, companies that guarantee you a result that sounds too good to be true are likely scammers. At minimum, they are lying to you by omission by leaving out the possibility that you may not get such a favorable offer. At worst, they may be planning to hit you with huge hidden fees after delivering a seemingly favorable initial outcome.

There are no guarantees that one can advertise in the debt relief area. Because each creditor and borrower is different, a company cannot know exactly what deal they will be able to negotiate for you until they actually understand your situation. Anyone promising to deliver a specific result in a specific amount of time before even starting the process is either confused or hiding something.

#4 Check the Credentials of the Company

The good news is, there are many ways to check the reputation and credentials of debt relief companies.

Organizations like the American Fair Credit Council (AFCC), the International Association of Professional Debt Arbitrators (IAPD), and the Receivable Management Association (RMA) all hold their members to specific standards of ethics, competence, and professionalism. Any organization offering debt relief should be a member of at least one of these organizations.

You can also see what kinds of experiences previous customers have had with a company by checking resources like its record with the Better Business Bureau.

Lastly, any debt relief organization offering you services should be licensed to operate in your state. Believe it or not, that can be an issue: debt relief laws vary from state to state, so just because a debt relief business operates successfully in a neighboring state does not necessarily mean they are licensed to legally operate in yours.

#5 Look for Video Testimonials

Unfortunately, the faking of written reviews has become a popular practice in recent years. Shady companies may even hire hundreds of "customers" and pay them a small fee to write fake reviews which may even fool third-party review verifiers in some cases.

However, it takes a lot more time, effort, and money to fake a video testimonial. Because it is so much more labor-intensive, companies rarely bother to fake these. This may change as AI-generated video gets cheaper and more photorealistic, but for now, video testimonials are much more likely to come from real customers than from paid actors.

#6 Consider Alternatives to Debt Relief

Debt relief services like these are not right for everyone. It's not just a matter of getting to pay less money with no consequences: using debt relief services can damage your credit, which will require time devoted to good financial behaviors to repair. So it's worth considering your individual circumstances: are debt relief services likely to damage your credit more or less than what you're already doing?

This is one of the questions we discuss in our free consultations at https://FreeDebtHelp.com.

Some other options you can consider instead of debt relief include:

- Debt consolidation. This is a service offered by many banks in which you take out a single loan which is sufficient to pay all your debts, and then pay it back to the bank at a fixed rate. This can be a better option for many people if they can afford the monthly payments on the loan, as it does not damage your credit score, and may even improve it if you make payments on time.

- With help from a financial planner or a piece of software, you may be able to find a way to pay all your debts without requiring debt relief. This, too, protects your credit history compared to bargaining for a reduced payoff amount.

- Some people may find filing for bankruptcy to be a better option if they are in severe, global financial distress. If your business has failed or another calamity has occurred that makes it totally impossible for you to pay your debts, bankruptcy may relieve you of more debt than debt relief services. It's best to consult with a financial professional before filing for bankruptcy, however, as bankruptcy does damage your credit history significantly.

If you think debt relief services might help you but you're not sure if they're the right option, we're happy to talk through your situation with you at https://FreeDebtHelp.com.

Chapter 8

How Can You Profit from Fintech While Blessing Others?

Throughout this book, we've discussed how fintech is transforming the way money moves around the country and the world. We've discussed how it can lower barriers to inequality, including through making business ownership more accessible. But you may also have noticed something: making new fintech products is *hard*. It often requires a level of technical expertise that most people simply don't have.

That's one reason I am such a big believer in the direct sales model to allow anyone to profit from offering financial services and technologies to others.

As we've seen throughout this book, the capabilities of fintech in realms including financial education, credit building, debt relief, and business training and mentorship, are truly transformative. I firmly believe that with these tools available, anyone who is dedicated to achieving a financial or business goal can obtain it. This includes the building of generational wealth.

Right now, the major obstacle to the empowerment of all people through fintech is simply lack of public awareness. The most empowering products are not necessarily those which are most aggressively promoted by big corporations, who perhaps would prefer that people continued to rely on them for employment and services instead of learning to be self-sufficient. So there is still a big lack of awareness that many of these fintech products even exist, or that they work.

This is how you can help, and how you can profit. Through direct selling of fintech services, you can start your own business selling fintech products that already exist.

The direct sales model, when combined with empowering fintech products, is a massive win/win/win. The inventor of the product receives a cut of the profits, you receive another cut of the profits as the seller, and the customer receives the necessary education and empowerment to build generational wealth for themselves.

As we bring this book to a close, I want to share with you some valuable tools for thinking about money that have helped me to build Novae, get it on the Inc 5000 for four years running, and shaped my philosophy and ethics around the products we sell.

We've spent most of this book discussing why fintech products are great for consumers, potentially including yourself. I think it's very important that we understand the power of these products and services to fight historic sources of inequality, regardless of our personal relationship to them.

But I also promised you that you could profit off of becoming involved in this business, even if you're not a software developer or a business guru. Now let's focus on discussing why direct sales is great for entrepreneurs and business owners, including yourself if you so choose.

Robert Kiyosaki's Cashflow Quadrants

Robert Kiyosaki is the author of the legendary book *Rich Dad, Poor Dad*, which discusses the attitudes and knowledge that rich families pass on to their children to help ensure they remain rich and even become richer. One of the key concepts he discusses is that of the "cashflow quadrants": a way of separating mindsets about money into four different categories based on the two dimensions of ownership and work.

These quadrants help explain why direct selling is such a powerful experience for reshaping a person's potential for financial success. The four quadrants are as follows:

1. In the first quadrant is the "E" quadrant, for "employee." In this quadrant, a person has a job.

   This is where the vast majority of people today sit: they have been given a job by an organization, and they are paid a salary, which is decided by someone else, for doing that job. Notice that people in this employee quadrant depend on two things to continue to make money: they must be given a job by someone else, and they must continue to work that job for as long as they wish to receive money.

2. In the second quadrant, called the "S" quadrant for "self-employed," a person creates their own job. In this quadrant, a person has taken one kind of power into their own hands: they create their own job, which gives them more freedom and probably higher pay than if their job depended on taking orders from an organization and splitting profits with said organization.

However, the self-employed person's earnings are still dependent on one very important factor: a self-employed person can only earn as much as they can work. They don't own anything that will create passive income for them if they lose the ability to work.

3. The third quadrant is the "B" quadrant, for "business owners." These are people who have built a *system* that pays them money. Because they are paid by a system that can function without them, not by a job, their income is not dependent on their ability to work.

The break between self-employed and business owner is not a clean one: a new business owner must spend years working to build their business system and making sure it runs properly or it will never function well enough to support them.

But business owners have the *potential* to collect passive income and wealth from their business that is not limited by how much they, personally, can work. By growing their business, such as by hiring more employees and introducing scalable products, they can grow their income more than would be possible if they could only profit off of their own personal labor.

4. The fourth quadrant is the "I" quadrant, for "investor." In this quadrant, a person already has a lot of money. They can now make that money make *more* money for them by investing it in stocks, bonds, and other people's businesses. Because they own value, they can essentially lend that value to other businesses and get paid a portion of the profit that other people's businesses make using their money.

This is truly passive income. Since other people are running the businesses that use their money, the investor does not *need* to be involved at all, except to watch their portfolio and ensure that their investments are still making money and not losing it. If their investments start losing money, they can simply move their money somewhere else.[1]

People who are really ambitious about building wealth want to plan to move from the earlier quadrants to the later ones. This stepwise progression is often necessary because of the skills and assets that are required to move up to the next class.

Employees may be able to leverage their employee skills and savings to become self-employed, but it will be challenging to jump immediately to being a successful business owner if they have no business experience.

A self-employed person can become a successful business owner, but most self-employed people will not have enough assets to jump immediately to making all of their income from investing.

A business owner can then become a successful investor after gaining enough wealth that their money can provide a full-time income through investment.

Each movement between quadrants requires a fundamental mindset shift. An employee must believe they have the power and the right to find their own work without a company bringing them clients and customers in order to become self-employed.

A self-employed person must believe they have the power and the right to build a system where their own employees generate money for them in order to become a business owner.

A business owner must believe that they have the right and ability to accrue a large amount of wealth before they are wealthy enough to join the investor quadrant.

Spending time in direct selling can directly facilitate the mindset shift from employee to self-employed to business owner, facilitating progress from one quadrant to the next more powerfully than any other education or experience I know of.

Direct selling teaches people to find their own customers, maximize their earnings from their own labor, and begin to build a network of other sellers whose work can create some income for them too. This model helps people move into the "B" quadrant faster than any other opportunity out there, in my opinion.

More importantly, it creates experiences of mastery in these areas which leave direct sellers like myself prepared to start their own infinitely scalable businesses and ultimately join the investor class.

Why Direct Selling is the Best Starter Business

In previous chapters, we've briefly discussed the steps necessary to start your own business. We've discussed the skills required to be successful, and the paradox that starting a business is both harder and easier than you think.

It's harder in that you need boots-on-the-ground experience with selling products and designing sales models to be successful, which few people receive in school or on the job as employees. It's easier in that you absolutely do not need a college or graduate degree.

Direct selling is the best business to start, in my opinion, because it immediately gives you experience with those hands-on aspects you didn't learn in school or as an employee taking orders, without requiring you to go through a huge process of inventing your own product line, marketing materials, business plan, etc.

As a direct seller, you are essentially handed a business plan that has worked for many other people in the past and told to execute it. You then get to keep most of the profits of your labor, and in the process of execution you gain hands-on knowledge of what is necessary for success in future business endeavors.

According to the Direct Selling Association, about 10% of Americans are customers of at least one direct sales business. 65% of direct sellers report that they value the business model because it offers them freedom and flexibility. 78% of direct sellers reported that they would recommend direct selling as a business model to others and said the experience had met or exceeded their expectations.[2]

I share these statistics with you because I want to make it clear to you how large the potential market for your direct selling business is, and how satisfied four out of five direct sellers are with their business model. But now let's dive more into discussing the direct sales business model and its benefits.

Benefits of Becoming a Direct Sales Entrepreneur

The benefits of being a direct sales entrepreneur often sound too good to be true to people who haven't done it before. But these

---

2. Direct Selling Association. (2019). *Direct Selling: An Accessible Path to Entrepreneurship*. Washington, DC; Direct Selling Association.

benefits really are not just realistic, but possible. These benefits are the reality for myself, my wife, and even the editor of this book who uses a similar business model to my own for her literary services. This world is out there, even though you might never have seen it if you've been a lifelong employee.

Benefit #1: Flexibility

For hundreds of millions of employees in the United States, the idea of making your own hours and working when you want to sounds too good to be true. Yet this is the reality of millions of business owners, including direct sales entrepreneurs.

This doesn't mean you never have to work: if you want to make large profits you will probably have to put in long hours, especially in the first few years of running your business. But it *does* mean that you don't have to ask a boss for time off, or worry about being late to work unless you've scheduled a specific appointment with someone else for that time.

You decide when you work and when you take time off, and you even get to decide how *much* you work depending on how much you want or need to earn. If you can make it work with the schedule you create with your customers and any other team members you may have, you can take any day or time off.

Benefit #2: Work From Home

This is true in many direct sales roles, but it is especially true in fintech where you don't need to go door to door putting on demonstrations of physical products. Because you are selling a digital product that customers can access from home, many meetings and most work can be conducted from the comfort of your own home with no need to commute or clock in at a certain time.

I do advise that direct sellers engage in *some* work outside the home, such as putting on educational events in their local communities. But the daily reality of your business is unlikely to involve having to leave your house at all, unless you want to.

For that matter, you can also do a lot of your work from your favorite coffee shop or vacation spot if you so choose. As long as you can work your schedule so that all meetings can be conducted online, you can travel as much as you want while still working.

Benefit #3: Minimal Investment

Most business opportunities are *expensive* to start up. While starting out in the direct sales industry will cost you something, it is one of the most affordable business models to start.

This is especially true if you are selling digital products like fintech products and services. If your products are digital, there will be no need for you to buy physical equipment or products to stock.

Most digital direct sales programs do charge a startup fee to cover the costs of your training and licensing you to sell their products. This is necessary since the company doesn't yet know if you will actually follow through and sell their products and they have invested significant time in putting on live trainings, creating training materials, and creating relationships of trust with partner businesses whose products you will also be licensed to sell.

However, some, like Novae's debt relief referral service, have no startup cost at all.

Benefit #4: Personal Growth

Very few jobs offer the same potential as direct sales for learning practical, versatile, and lucrative on-the-job skills. In many jobs you will learn respectable skills, but most of these don't involve learning to become a successful small business owner.

To become a successful business owner, you must usually know how to craft and optimize a business plan, how to perform sales and marketing, how to communicate clearly at an advanced level, and much more. These are all skills that are learned and practiced daily in direct sales. The experience of success as a direct sales entrepreneur will give you not only the skills, but also the confidence to subsequently create and promote your own businesses in the future.

The skills learned in direct sales can be applied to running a business in almost any industry. These are the skills that are missing from what you learn in *most* jobs, which often teach the technical skills required for their industry but not the business skills necessary to make business decisions, create strong sales, and ultimately run a successful business of your own.

In that sense, direct sales skills are an excellent complement to any sort of educational or professional background. You will get practice running your own direct sales business, which will give you much of the confidence, knowledge, and habits that you need to sell any kind of product and run any kind of business in the future.

In fact, my wife and I both worked in direct sales in a few different industries before starting Novae. Once we learned how to optimize our sales and cash flow, we were able to move between different industries, selecting the products and services we wanted to sell according to what would meet our needs best.

I ultimately started Novae using my skills from the direct sales industry after I learned about financial technology and concluded that it was the best business for blessing both my own family and my customers.

Benefit #5: Build Confidence

Too often, the culture of the workplace is one of uncertainty and fear. Managers and owners often distrust employees and fear that they will not make the right decisions or act responsibly. This often leaves people who have only worked as employees feeling uncertain of their abilities to succeed on their own, without a boss or manager, and lacking in the confidence needed to successfully promote their own businesses.

In direct sales, you will have daily experiences of success. At first the level of responsibility you have for your own success will feel terrifying to some, and initial failures to sell or communicate may feel daunting.

But that is the value of the direct sales industry. We only overcome these fears and weaknesses by powering through them. We only gain these skills, and we only get better and gain the confidence that we actually are very, very good at what we do and have good judgment through hands-on experience of success.

In the direct sales industry, you will be surrounded by people who want you to succeed, and who know that you can do it. The independence of this business model means that no one *wants* to micromanage you: they want you to succeed on your own. And they have probably seen people with much weaker starting skills than your own do so, if they only stick to the process of learning and growing by doing. Most people get started for themselves, but in this industry you're not alone because your success is the success of the person that introduced and enrolled you with the direct selling company.

It has been my experience that confidence is possibly *the* most important ingredient in business success. Obviously, you also need to be able to run a financially solvent operation, but to be honest, it's easier to succeed in business and finance with confidence and *without* technical competence than it is to succeed if you are the most technically competent person in the world but you lack confidence in your abilities as a businessperson.

This is one benefit that, to be frank, is almost impossible to find anywhere else. There are very few settings in adult life that are specifically designed to teach you the skills and confidence you need to run a business with encouragement from more knowledgeable and experienced mentors.

As someone who has attended both, I can say that even most business graduate schools do not offer the same level of training in confidence and independence as direct sales organizations.

Benefit #6: Uncapped Income

In a direct sales network or as an independent business owner, your earning potential is theoretically limitless. While again, it takes *work* to obtain these earnings, you are not constricted by a fixed salary that an employer has assigned as the value of your work. Instead your earnings are limited only by the products and services you can sell.

This is a double-edged sword: no maximum salary cap *also* means no minimum guaranteed salary. Direct sales is typically a commission-only business. But for someone who is highly motivated to succeed in this industry, the earning potential is often higher as a direct seller than as an hourly employee in most professions.

If you want to become a millionaire, it's much easier to do that if you have business and sales skills than by trying to use the skills of almost any other profession. And even though most direct sellers don't become millionaires, direct sellers *do* have a higher average income than the average American.[3]

Benefit #7: Join a Community

As a direct seller with a reputable organization, you'll be joining a community of people who are interested in each other's success. In this industry, your colleagues aren't just people you're forced to be in the office with every day: they're people who have actively chosen the same path as you, and who have chosen to attend industry events.

Building community ties, like anything else, takes work. But by becoming a direct seller, you'll be joining a community of like-minded individuals with the potential to form strong bonds.

What to Look for in Your First Direct Sales Company

Unfortunately, it's no secret these days that some direct selling companies have a bad reputation. I won't name names because I'm not here to gossip, but you might have heard that some companies have been accused of misleading sellers and customers in an effort to get paid lots of money for low-value or even fraudulent products. It would be a disservice to everyone involved to pretend this is not a concern when considering entering the direct selling

---

3. Direct Selling Association. (2019). *Direct Selling: An Accessible Path to Entrepreneurship*. Washington, DC; Direct Selling Association.

industry. There is a general stigma against the Direct Selling industry, that many of the companies are pyramid schemes or Ponzi schemes. Most people that make these accusations are simply uneducated on the industry, or may only have heard the worst stories of bad behavior that have appeared in the headlines.

As with most business models, there have been scammers who have used the direct selling model to deceive or coerce potential sellers. That's why I want to give you a list of red and green flags to use to decide whether a specific direct selling company is likely to benefit you. I want to reassure you that I sold and consulted for several direct selling companies prior to Novae, and my experiences were so good that I decided to make direct selling the basis of my own company. But as with any industry, the direct selling industry is not immune to bad actors.

So how can you know if a company that offers direct selling opportunities will treat you well and really help your customers? Here are a few recommendations I have.

Look to Sell a Product You Believe In

One common point of controversy around direct sales companies is whether their products really have as much value as advertised. Certain direct selling companies in the wellness industry, for example, have been accused of exaggerating the claims of their products' effectiveness and subsequently leaving sellers with less valuable products than what they thought they would be selling when they signed up.

Look for companies that are clear and enthusiastic about the value of their product, yet whose claims are realistic and supported by customer experiences. A juice that claims to cure cancer, a pill that brings youth, or a bot that earns you millions in the stock market in your sleep, could all be discussed to get you to invest, yet upon examination it's likely that none of these products are actually yielding those results for their customers.

In some cases, the question of whether a product or company actually does what it claims might not be obvious. So how do you vet products or companies before joining one?

Beware of Pyramid and Ponzi Schemes

When people are recruiting other people to pay money to join a "company" and there is no real product or service being sold, this is where you should steer clear. If there is no product that has been proven to add real value to the marketplace, the company may indeed be a Ponzi or pyramid scheme.

Bernie Madoff scammed the wealthy out of billions of dollars on Wall Street by claiming to invest the money they gave him in a portfolio that never existed. He claimed he could get investors fabulously, unrealistically high returns on their investments.

Instead, he would pay out "returns on investment" to his early investors using some of the money that new investors gave him to convince people that the investment opportunity was real. Then he'd keep the rest of the money to spend himself, so later investors lost all the money they gave him. This is the very definition of a

Ponzi scheme.

Any industry can fall prey to this sort of scheme. The biotech company Theranos took in almost a billion dollars from would-be customer and investors before it became clear that their miracle diagnostic technology never actually existed. Someone with a skeptical scientific eye might have guessed that the technology they promised was too good to be true, but thousands of people assumed that if others believed in the company, then it must be telling the truth.

With all things, in business and in life, use your common sense. If a product or service sounds way too good to be true, it probably is. And if the product is bad, you may lose money or even get into trouble for selling it.

Research the Word of Mouth

Even something as simple as searching "is _____ a good company?" can yield enlightening results. Searches like this will often turn up numerous third party review sites and even news articles about the company you're researching. In this way you'll learn if they've had any scandals, if regulatory authorities have expressed concern about their practices, and how satisfied their sellers and customers generally are.

Remember that *all* companies will have some 1-star reviews. Despite our best efforts, no company yields great results 100% of the time, and people are most likely to leave reviews if they've had a bad experience. Still, you may find some very stark differences between the companies you're researching. If one company is rated much more highly than others, or one company is the subject of numerous news articles about potentially harmful practices, you have your answer.

Asking your own social network is even better. If you know people who have worked for these companies, they are probably an even better source of information than online reviews which may be faked or biased. If someone you know is claiming that they had a really good or really bad experience with a direct selling company, listen carefully. They have valuable lived experience on this subject.

Just as with print media, consider the source when receiving word-of-mouth recommendations. Is the person giving you the feedback someone who has had success in many endeavors and whose judgment you generally trust? Or are they someone who has a habit of starting projects and not finishing them, or who has hated every job they've ever worked?

I like to say that when many people complain about one company, it's probably the company that's the problem. But when one person complains about many companies, that might not be the case.

I hate that I even need to say this, but in this day and age we must even be aware of potential conflicts of interest by review websites.

When searching "Is Novae a good company?" for myself, for example, I found one website that claimed few Novae sellers experienced success—but the review website's sidebar was literally an advertisement where the owners of the review website claimed you could make $10,000 per month using *their* system.

This made it clear that the website owners would profit directly from convincing people to avoid Novae (and all other direct selling companies) and sign up for their own program instead.

This brings me to my next red flag...

Be Wary of Astounding or Specific Guarantees

Responsible business educators will make it clear to their direct sellers that the sellers' pay will be dependent on their own level of effort and skill, and may take a while to grow. This isn't hedging: it's being truthful about how all businesses work. As I've mentioned before, anyone promising "effortless" or "guaranteed" money is probably misleading you.

The ad I saw on the review website, for example, strongly implied that anyone could make more than $10,000 per month using their system. When I clicked on this ad, the sales page then claimed that the author was making $40,000 per month using the system. While both of these statements may be true—it may be *possible* for anyone to make $10,000 per month—these statements contained absolutely no information about *how* the system worked, or what kind of skills, effort, and startup capital would be required to accomplish that level of success.

Flashing promises of earning specific dollar amounts is a common way for people using high-pressure sales tactics to mislead or pressure you into making a decision in favor of their company, so be wary when these kinds of figures pop up. It doesn't automatically mean they're lying, but it does suggest that they're willing to raise your expectations high before even discussing the work involved with you.

On a related note…

Beware of Companies Claiming to Know "Secret" Techniques

Many ads will claim to teach you to make passive income using a "secret trick" that "no one knows about." This is a red flag because it's a way to convince you to believe questionable promises.

When someone promises that you can make thousands of dollars per month in just a few hours of work per week, for example, your natural response is probably, "That doesn't sound realistic: if it were, everyone would do it!" The company pre-empts this doubt by explaining that "no one knows" about this technique, and that's why you've never heard of it before.

Let's be realistic: if you are being advertised a training course, then the course is not a "secret." It is very public and probably being shown to thousands to millions of people each day. That doesn't mean there is no potential for profit, but it does mean that you should treat anything else the company says with a grain of salt because, again, they have already shown a willingness to make questionable claims to get your interest.

Look for Companies That Align With Your Core Values

What are your core values? What kind of difference do you want to make in the world? How would you run a business to be in line with your own ethics and morality?

Once you have answered those questions, look for a company that gives the same answers. And look for companies that don't just *say* the right things, but actually do them in practice. To find out if this is the case, you can research word of mouth like we suggested before. See how current sellers and customers say they have been treated by the company. Look to see what educational, charity, and community service initiatives the company has.

If available, listen to the founder's story and the professed mission of the company. If one founder focuses on talking about how great it is to have luxury yachts and sports cars while another focuses on how their product helps customers to better their lives, that may be an important piece of information. Which founder more reflects what you want to achieve in your own life? Which do you trust more to treat you well as a seller or customer?

If you have the opportunity to attend a networking event for these businesses, you can also learn about the "vibe" of the company as a community there. Do you feel welcome and supported, and do people seem generally supportive of each other? Or does something feel "off," like the people might have values you don't share?

A supportive direct selling community is an amazing thing to belong to. Such a community can help shift you into the business owner quadrant and prepare you to transform the future of generational wealth for your family. But an unhealthy community can encourage you to drain yourself dry to support the company, or even shame and blame you if you struggle to succeed. Which type of community does the company you're researching feel like?

External accolades and acceptances like industry credentials, membership in reputable industry organizations, and awards from outside organizations is also a good sign that a company walks the walk of providing value and behaving ethically. The third-party organizations that bestow these credentials, memberships, and awards have reputations of their own to uphold, so they are unlikely to tolerate or reward organizations that are badly behaved.

In general, the better a company's reputation, the better your reputation will be as a seller. So picking a company that is widely accepted and awarded by other organizations is a good way to make sure that sterling reputation transfers to you as a seller.

Look for Companies that Respect Your Intelligence

I'll be honest: having nuanced, honest discussions is not always the best way to make money in this day and age. In fact, it rarely is: sadly, many companies resort to misleading or questionable marketing claims because they *work*. Many people will uncritically accept what they are told and view complex discussions as a sign of weakness or uncertainty.

Despite this, I believe it's important to be honest with people and not feed into the culture of doing anything to sell your product. If a company truly wishes to set its sellers up for lifelong success in business, it must be honest with them about the skills and labor required to become a successful business owner.

Making the process sound "easy," "quick," or "effortless" is the opposite of helpful: those are *not* truths in the real life business world, and are really only useful for helping the recruiting company to make an "easy, quick, and effortless" buck off of the aspiring entrepreneur.

Look for companies and coaches that are honest with you. Being a successful business owner is hard work, at least for the first few years when you are building your skills, referral base, and product catalog. Being a successful business owner is arguably *harder* than any other job, at least for those first few years.

The level of skill, effort, and responsibility required is unparalleled. This is what people need to expect if they are to be truly successful and independent business people.

Of course there's a *reason* why people like myself, my wife, and all of my thousands of students, partners, and affiliates choose this path. It's because once you have built those skills and that referral base, you have a job with unparalleled freedom and higher earning potential than any other job title. As a business owner, your pay is only limited by how much you can scale, and your ability to scale is only limited by your skill and foresight.

This is an ideal position to be in, especially in a time of great change and financial uncertainty. This is the position I want *you* to be in. That's why I wrote this book.

Chapter 9

How Can Fintech Reshape the Future?

We live in an era where wealth inequality and affordability are growing concerns. As many industries seem priced to extract wealth from most people and many industries are looking to replace workers with AI, it's natural to feel anxiety. And there is some wisdom in this anxiety: now is the time, more than any other in recent memory, to take our financial futures into our own hands.

Fortunately, it is also easier than it has ever been to start your own business and keep more of the profits of your own labor, instead of relying on an employer for a paycheck. Technologies that allow people to work and conduct business from anywhere in the world mean that our access to finance is no longer dependent on our geographic location or our ability to travel.

In this era where we watch billionaires get richer and most people struggle, it is still possible for us to become wealthy and financially independent. It isn't *easy*, but it starts with taking our financial destinies into our own hands through education, addressing issues blocking us from accessing the financial system, and ultimately developing a business owner mindset that values our time and our skills sufficiently to get us paid what we're worth.

Used ethically, fintech has the potential to equalize access to financial education, giving the children of the poor and middle classes the same kind of knowledge about how to make money as the children of the rich.

Fintech has the potential to increase access to capital, removing many barriers that have previously made people who aren't members of the favored class, culture, race, and religion much less likely to receive the kind of financing that business owners from wealthy families take for granted.

Fintech even has the potential to help ease the debt crisis for some. Although the debt crisis ultimately needs systemic laws and policies to stop wealth extraction from the poor and the middle classes, the new models of debt relief can make the process a little bit kinder for debtors than the traditional methods of for-profit debt collectors.

I believe that as technology advances and jobs are lost to automation, measures like universal healthcare, universal basic income, and regulations on the pricing of goods that are essential for survival will be needed to create a long-term future for our children.

Many of us are already doing all we can to make that happen, by showing up to city council meetings, getting involved in activist organizations and mutual aid networks, and voting for politicians who support expanding lifesaving public services.

You can read more about some of my proposals to benefit the Black community in my book, *The Plan After Police Reform*. While that book focuses on cultural as well as financial factors impacting the Black community, many of the exercises in its companion workbook, *The Plan Workbook*, can benefit anyone from a lower- or middle-income background as they focus on personal and community exercises you can do to get involved in changing your mindset and making policy.

But one thing is clear: we can't afford to wait for legislative change. Knowledgeable people have been asking for it for decades, and it still isn't here. So now is the time to take matters into our own hands. We must build our own financial foundations through education, action, and ideally building the mindset of a business owner who knows how to turn their skills and products into cash flow without the need for an employer or a boss.

A great deal of the business owner mindset *is* about valuing your time and skills. As employees and students we are taught to accept the salaries we are offered and follow orders. We are often made to feel inadequate, and to question our ability to get by without our employer or boss.

They keys to success as a business owner include being highly effective in communicating our value, negotiating our own prices for our services, and creating and executing our own business plan for which we get to keep most profits. And I know of no better way to learn those skills quickly and effectively than as part of a community of direct sellers.

I've been tremendously blessed since I discovered direct selling, and not just with financial benefits. I find the person that I have become in the process much more valuable. I now have a sense of radical responsibility for my life, but also a sense of radical confidence. Experience has taught me that I can solve problems and create plans that succeed without needing to rely on an employer or a boss.

Of course, I also credit much of my personal development to my faith. My grandfather, Paw Paw, was my father figure growing up, and he was a remarkable man. A pastor in a Black church, he firmly believed that God would provide—and that God intended us to provide for others. He taught me to work hard with hope and optimism, and keep a keen eye out for God's blessings when they came into my life.

He also taught me that "to whom much is given, from him much will be expected." The Bible isn't talking about cash when it says this: instead, the parable is about using God's blessings to do good in the world. Having faith in more than material wealth has kept me grounded, disciplined and focused on my God-given purpose.

I've been incredibly blessed. That means if I want to be judged favorably, I'd better do a heck of a lot of good! I hope my readers will share that philosophy, regardless of what religious or ethical text you take the idea from.

Let's all make the world a better place together.

About the Author

Reco McCambry has been married to Shaneé since 2007 and has 3 children, Reco Jr., Raegan, and Rylee. He has made his mark in the fintech and direct sales industry as one of the youngest and most successful entrepreneurs in the space. His company, Novae, is the largest direct sales fintech company in the United States, providing greater access to credit, capital, and entrepreneurship to underserved communities nationwide through a network of thousands of independent salespeople.

Reco is a member of the Forbes Business Council and Industry Expert on Forbes.com. He also serves on the National Small Business Association Leadership Council out of Washington DC. He's been selected to the #1 Business Honor Society in the world, Beta Gamma Sigma after earning a 4.0 GPA in one of the nation's top MBA programs.

Novae has been recognized by Inc. magazine, Inc 5000, as one of the fastest growing companies in America, four years in a row (2021 - 2024) ranking number 903 at its highest. Novae ranked in the top 60 fastest growing financial services companies in the US most recently while ranking in the top 50 fastest growing companies in Georgia.

On February 4, 2021, Mr. McCambry was honored by his

ABOUT THE AUTHOR

hometown in McDonough, GA with a proclamation naming January 19th, Mr. Reco McDaniel McCambry Day. In 2022, McCambry was named Innovator of the Year at the Bank Customer Service Summit, received the Outstanding Leadership Award at the Money 2.0 Conference, and in 2023 Coles College of Business at Kennesaw State University named him Graduate of the Last Decade.

www.ingramcontent.com/pod-product-compliance
Lightning Source LLC
Chambersburg PA
CBHW051947290426
44110CB00015B/2137